Whatever You Do

(SIX FOUNDATIONS)

For An Integrated Life

Edited by Luke Bobo

Cover design and creative direction: Eric Rivier
Interior design: Daniel Carroll

ISBN 9781093754254

Printed in the United States of America
First Edition

Contents

Introduction

Several years ago, my wife and I visited a church and began talking to an older woman after the service. Knowing I was a pastor, the woman asked my wife, "And what do you do? Are you employed at the church too?" It was an innocent question, but one that was loaded.

My wife, a finance major with eight years of corporate experience answered, "I work at an insurance brokerage that helps companies assess financial risk and find insurance solutions. I'm in sales, and we sell solutions like directors' and officers' insurance to nursing homes."

A blank stare. You could tell the gears in the woman's head were temporarily frozen. In an improvisational moment, she replied, "Well that's nice — you can probably lead your coworkers in Bible studies and share the gospel with them."

The implications of this conversation were that my wife's work only held meaning insofar as it led to the real work of ministry — Bible studies and evangelism.

My wife recovered. "I actually see the work I do every day as my primary ministry. When I'm doing good work, I am living out my calling."

Two women. Two different paradigms of ministry. Two different understandings about what it means to serve God. Two different conceptions of what God is doing in the world, and how a woman like my wife might participate in it.

For the past several decades, there has been a growing movement of Christians who are thinking deeply about integrating faith with how they spend a majority of their time — at work, whether paid or unpaid. But there persists a deep misunderstanding about how everyday work and participation in the economy relates to God's mission in the world.

For instance, consider these statistics gathered by Barna: Only 28% of Christian workers are seeking to actively integrate their faith with their work.[1] And 73% of practicing Christians say a pastor's vocation is more important than their own.[2]

Why is this the case? The reasons are complex. But I believe one of the chief reasons is that many of our beliefs, attitudes, and deepest held values lack coherence.

Coherence happens when one can look at all the parts, find logical consistency, and fit them together into a meaningful whole.

All of our beliefs, attitudes, and deepest held values are complex systems that have been shaped through many years of listening to teaching, admiring exemplars, inhabiting practices, and being formed by different communities. We rarely think about how the scaffolding has come to be, or of what influence it has over us. For most of us, this scaffolding has been built with areas of belief that are not integrated. Our beliefs often lack coherence.

For example, we may believe the Bible. We may love the Bible. But we may not possess a coherent reading of the Bible that affirms what God is doing from the first page to the last. We may not have thought deeply about how salvation in Christ is connected to God's first great commission, the cultural mandate to bear fruit and multiply. We may not have considered how our embodied existence in a renewed heavens and earth has any connection with our everyday work in this world. We know it matters when a soul is restored. Does it matter when a building is restored? This may seem like an arcane, academic exercise. It is not.

As Victor Frankl has explained in *Man's Search for Meaning*, we are meaning-seeking creatures. We want to know how our time and our energy has purpose and is part of a bigger story. Most of us are not medical missionaries, keeping dying people alive in third world countries. Most of our days are not spent evangelizing clients or bosses or coworkers. We mop floors. We fix cars. We restock grocery shelves. We answer emails. We lead recurring meetings. These mundane tasks can lead to a crisis of purpose. We lack coherence.

It is becoming more common for Christian leaders of many stripes to rightly decry the sacred versus secular divide. But the sacred/secular divide has unseen roots, like a weed that is cut down but lives out of sight. For instance, while we may agree that we shouldn't have a sacred/spiritual divide, we might unknowingly hold a spiritual versus material divide, a soul versus body divide, a for-profit versus non-profit divide, or an individual salvation versus cosmic renewal of all things divide.

This book explores how we can pursue a more coherent life and faith in six important areas. We believe that when these areas are woven together, they form a scaffolding that can help us live meaningful lives, or make meaning of our lives, which is a fundamental human need.

Chapter one will explore the unified story of the Bible, how God's creation relates to the profound disruption and disintegration of our world, to how God is making all things new and will one day finally unite heaven and earth.

Chapter two will trace God's mission through the entire Bible, focusing on his purposes in creation, his people Israel, Jesus Christ, and in and through his church. Did his plan for Adam and Eve have anything to do with his plan for Abraham? How does Jesus extend God's purposes in the creation mandate, and how might the church continue the work of Abraham?

Chapter three explores how formation in Christ impacts the whole person. Rather than isolating the spiritual from the material or the body from the soul, a coherent anthropology has profound implications for how we envision apprenticeship to Jesus, as we are "renewed in the image of our creator," (Col 3:10). And how can local churches apply this understanding as they seek to make disciples of all nations?

Chapter four will explore a coherent view of work. How do we think about both the intrinsic value of work alongside of the extrinsic value of work? And what counts as service to God? The one-off bits where we are specifically talking about our faith with others, or the large bulk of our time that is spent doing what our employer hired us to do?

Chapter five will move from the "me" of faith and work to the "we" of our participation in the broader economy. Specifically, does our faith have coherence with the fact that we are economic actors in a global marketplace? What do market based strategies and outcomes have to do with loving our neighbors, and loving the "least of these?"

Finally, chapter six will explore the role of the local church in the world. Are the purposes of the church at odds with how most congregation members spend most of their time, or are they coherent? How can the mission of the church uphold the goodness of the gathered community while also promoting and empowering the scattered church throughout the week?

Each of these chapters can be read in isolation, as each one was written by a different author, and makes an argument that can stand on its own. But the chapters themselves also have an internal coherence. Taken together, they form the theological scaffolding to make meaning of all of life and form a philosophy of ministry that values whole life discipleship. It could help a pastor not only tell a carpenter that God's first call on his life was to make good tables (as Dorothy Sayers argues in her essay, *Why Work?*), but also provide the theological reasons why.

This book was written for pastors and their churches. Made to Flourish exists to empower pastors and their churches to integrate faith, work, and economics for the flourishing of their communities. It is also written for anyone who is seeking to make sense of their lives in view of what God calls us to. It is written for anyone who longs for coherence in a bifurcated world. We hope it is a resource that can lead you "further up and further in" as you seek to live all of life as unto the Lord.

Matt Rusten
Executive Director, Made to Flourish

The Bible's Big Story:
How the Grand Narrative Informs Our Lives and Directs Our Mission

AMY L. SHERMAN

GETTING THE BOOKENDS RIGHT

A pair of wooden elephant bookends sit proudly on my fireplace mantle. When I see them, I recall my 2010 trip to Kenya. I also think of the Bible, thanks to a lecture I heard Andy Crouch give a few years ago. Andy suggested the functional theology for many Christians starts in Genesis 3 with the fall and ends in Revelation 20 with the great judgment. We have the bookends in the wrong place, reducing the Bible's story of creation, fall, redemption, and consummation to fall and redemption only. And the consequences are weighty.

The fall-redemption paradigm captures central biblical truth. It teaches us that humans are sinful and need a Savior, which God sent as an act of lavish grace. By sending his own holy Son to live the life we should have lived and die the death we should have died, God repaired our fellowship with him. He made it possible for us to gain eternal life.

This beautiful and true gospel, though, is incomplete. The Bible's big story starts with creation in Genesis 1 and ends with the consummation of Christ's kingdom in Revelation 22. Without the bookends in their proper place, we will not give God all the honor he deserves. We will not fully grasp our calling to live out our discipleship in every arena of life. We will not fully understand what obedience to the great requirement (Mic 6:8), the great commandment (Mark 12:29-31), or the great commission (Matt 28:19-20) looks like.

When our functional theology is truncated to only two installments of the Bible's four-chapter story, we risk thinking that "saving souls" is the believer's only vocation, our only calling. But when the bookends are in their proper position, we see our vocations expand beyond the work of evangelism, yet still including it. When we understand the big story, we gain clarity on living an integrated, missional life.

CREATION

The big story starts with God, not with us (a radical idea in today's culture). It begins with Trinitarian love: the three persons of the Godhead in blissful, satisfying communion. The world and human race join the scene as a result of this love. God creates a world to display his beauty and creates people to enjoy and participate in the love of the divine community.

Have you ever heard someone's anguished cry of "What are we here for, anyway?" The creation chapter gives us the two most important answers.

First, it tells us we're here for relationship. God made us for communion with himself, with each other, and with creation. Our primary call is to know, love, and be loved by him. But we're also called to a loving, human community: There are no rugged individualists or Lone Rangers in paradise. God's norm is a world of interdependent beings who are dependent on him. Creation depicts what the Hebrews termed shalom: the flourishing, or "webbing together of God, humans, and all

Without the bookends in their proper place, we will not give God _all the honor he deserves_.

creation in justice, fulfillment, and delight."[3]

Second, we're here for work that honors God and serves others. God created humankind in his own image, sharing with us the delight of being mini-creators. He set us in a creation that both meets our needs and also needs us (Gen 2:5). God, the choir director of the endless stars (Job 38:7), imbued us with abilities to organize, categorize, develop, interpret, and nurture. He set Adam and Eve free in the garden with the charge to tend and care for it: good work to enjoy and find satisfaction in.

Thus, we see how work is both good and normative. It's not a result of the fall. It's part of God's design. God intends human work to be a vehicle through which we express creativity, honor our maker, and serve one another. As we accomplish the cultural mandate (Gen 1:28, 2:15) we bear God's image in the world.

The creation narrative also shows us the ways things are meant to be. Everything is set right; everything is how God wants it. His world is one of love and goodness, flourishing and abundance, beauty and joy, freedom and responsibility, work and rest, development and preservation.

And, as the account teaches us, this is all a gift. Humans did not make this world. We did not make ourselves. As a familiar liturgy puts

If only the Bible –
in the paradise
But as we all
and Eve refused
dance of love

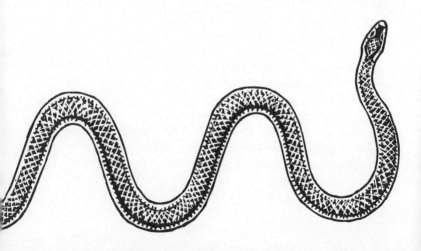

→ story could linger
of Genesis 1-2.
know, Adam
to join the *divine*
on God's terms.

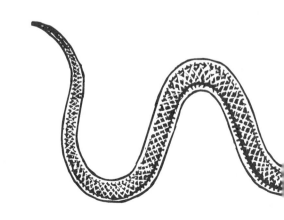

AMY L. SHERMAN

it: "It is he who has made us, and not we ourselves." We are not, as the commercial for Lincoln Financial puts it, our "own Life CEO." We own nothing in creation: God alone made it. Every good and perfect gift is from above (James 1:17).

The creation story also reveals our true identity. We are created beings, made in God's image, endowed with dignity. We need not seek elsewhere — in success, status, money, or sex — for our longed-for sense of "being okay." God handcrafted us in love. We can experience wholeness in remembering and embracing the twin realities of our glorious potential and our human finitude. This frees us to rest in this frenzied world of unbridled ambition.

FALL

If only the Bible story could linger in the paradise of Genesis 1-2. But as we all know, Adam and Eve refused to join the divine dance of love on God's terms. They chose to walk away from God's gracious invitation to be with him and to work with him. They tried to put themselves on the universe's throne rather than acknowledging their loving creator's rightful place. And this rebellion inaugurated profound, extensive, and devastating terrors.

The Bible's second chapter, the fall, shows us how sin permeates every aspect of shalom. In place of peace with God there is now alienation. Instead of calm self-acceptance, we are plagued with shame and psychological instability. Instead of loving, human communion, we are marked by hostility, suspicion, enmity, and violence. Consider, for example, America's high divorce rate or the fact that a report of child abuse is made every 10 seconds. In place of harmony and delight with the created order, there is now decay, corruption, brokenness, and death. Think of the BP oil spill, or of the latest person you heard has cancer. In place of Eden's paradise, we find ourselves in exiled wilderness.

And in the wilderness, we hate, kill, cry, and toil. In a world marked by the fall, everything falls apart. Relationships are shattered; humans are fragmented; bodies are torn; the earth is scarred.

Human selfishness even becomes institutionalized, bringing greater levels of oppression and injustice. Not only human hearts but human societies are corrupted.

In our individualistic culture, the privileged can sometimes fail to see this. The haves accuse the have-nots of failures of personal responsibility, as if this alone can explain the differences between the wealthy and the poor. Those in the majority are often blind to institutionalized racism and discrimination, seeing political, economic, and cultural systems as "neutral."

The relationships for which we were made — once sweet and deep — are now often fragile and fraught with tension. In this broken world, we experience belonging and betrayal, acceptance and rejection, fidelity and abandonment. Moreover, the work that once brought unstinting joy is now tainted with toil and futility. Sometimes we can feel satisfaction in our craft or enjoy the blessing of working in ways that draw upon our unique gifts. Other times labor is alienating, and many feel a sense of powerlessness, working as cogs in a machine whose purpose eludes them.

In the affluent West, the better-off can sometimes forget these truths. The culture around us promises youth, beauty, romance, and pleasure that we feel entitled to toil-less jobs, stress-free relationships, and age-defying bodies. Such misguided expectations explain some of our high rates of divorce, suicide, and disgruntlement with work.

GLIMPSES OF REDEMPTION
From the wailing of Genesis 3 to the opening cheer of New Testament Christmas, we see glimpses of the big story's third chapter — redemption — even amidst the ongoing aftershocks of the fall. On one hand, this section of the story stings us with the realities of our seemingly unending idolatries. We humans turn repeatedly from the spring of living water and try to quench our thirst for life, love, identity, meaning, purpose, beauty, and joy in all kinds of false and broken cisterns (Jer 2:13).

Yet on the other hand, consoling notes cut into this minor-key dirge as God pursues, forgives, renews, and restores. From the beginning, he promises a redeemer who will crush evil (Gen 3:15). He sews protective garments for his exiled children (Gen 3:21). He renews the world after the flood and re-commissions humans with their cultural mandate (Gen 8). He calls forth a new people for himself whom he will bless and make a blessing (Gen 12). He rescues those people from slavery in Egypt (Exod 12). He provides the Law, a prescription for how his people can live to attain a measure of shalom in the broken world (Exod 31). Over and over again he restores his wayward sons and daughters.

Old Testament narratives remind us of the insidiousness of human sin. Yet it is cleared-eye recognition of sin's pervasiveness that enables us to grasp the superlative power and wonder of redemption.

REDEMPTION

Though Israel failed in their calling from the Lord to build a society that could serve as a light to the nations, pointing people to God's justice and goodness, God sent his Son to be the light. God's long-promised plan of redemption was not thwarted by Israel's unfaithfulness. Jesus Christ came to stand as the perfect Israel, the perfect Adam, the perfect image-bearer.

With Jesus' incarnation and ministry, the kingdom of God broke into our time and space in new ways. Jesus announced his kingdom is here and now. He demonstrated its reality with all manner of miracles and healings. Jesus pushed back the curse and welcomed in the light.

When Jesus called the 12 disciples in Mark 3:13-15, we hear an echo from the creation story: God's invitation to be with him and to work with him. Now the work had a renewing flavor. The king was present in his creation, bringing renewal. C.S. Lewis' Narnia story, The Lion, The Witch and the Wardrobe, captures this well in the account of Aslan's arrival: The winter snow begin to melt, and spring begins to blossom. Jesus' breadth empowered his followers to participate in this work of renewal.

It is a holistic work, because the corruptions from the fall are not only "spiritual." Jesus both preached the living, true Word and healed broken bodies. He taught and he fed. He disrupted systems of injustice (e.g., the temple cleansing in Matthew 21:12-13). He upended both Herod's and Rome's ways of deploying power. He healed psychological and emotional wounds as well as physical traumas. He broke down ethnic and gender barriers. He practiced inclusion; he touched lepers; he broke bread with tax collectors; he loved his enemies. On the cross, Jesus repaired all four of the foundational relationships of shalom: peace with God, self, others, and the creation itself. Jesus' redemption is as broad as sin's curse.

Thus, the redeemer's invitation to participate in his mission involves our working in the power of the Holy Spirit for the renewal of all things. As disciples, our charge is to evangelize and to heal. It is to proclaim truth and to rescue the oppressed. It is to "teach others to obey all that Jesus taught" (Matt 28:20) and to imitate Jesus' deeds of compassion. It is to obey the social ethics of the Sermon on the Mount; to be life-givers in a culture of death and peace-makers in a violent world.

Jesus is renewing lawyers and the law; nurses and healthcare; engineers and engineering; politicians and politics.

We're living in this third chapter of the Bible's big story. We're living in the age of redemptive history where "Aslan (Jesus) is on the move;" where the Holy Spirit has been poured out onto the Church; where Satan's kingdom has been dismantled. The Church since its earliest days in the first century AD has been an initiator of personal and societal transformation. Scores, then hundreds, and then thousands of individuals came to find new life in the good news of Jesus. And the Church became the founder of the hospital. The Church was arguably the founder of the modern university. In Medieval times the Church played a key role in peacemaking. Perhaps the most famous example is when Pope Leo the Great rode out to confront Attila the Hun and persuaded him to spare Rome, which he did. Evangelicals like William Wilberforce and his friends from Clapham played a vital role in the overthrow of the British slave trade. In the 1830s, other British Evangelicals — notably Richard Oastler, George Bull, Michael Sadler — led the charge to abolish child labor.

The Church's mission of personal and societal renewal takes on different expressions in different ages but should never lose its holistic character. Because we are ambassadors of the whole gospel, we work for both the reconciliation of people to God and of people groups to one another — across racial, ethnic, gender, and religious divides. Because God made the world and called it good, and Jesus came to redeem the world, Christians must eschew the tendency to wall off a so-called "sacred" sphere from an allegedly inferior "secular" sphere. Jesus is redeeming all things and accepts no sacred/secular divide. There is "no square inch" over which king Jesus does not claim ownership. Jesus is renewing lawyers and the law; nurses and healthcare; engineers and engineering; politicians and politics. Jesus' renewing work dives deep into the individual's soul and stretches beyond the farthest reaches of the cosmos. He is making all peoples, all professions, all places new.

Today Christ-followers are participating in this work of renewal by promoting greater flourishing in workplaces. As a result of preaching he heard at his Episcopal church, Bob Chapman, CEO of Barry Wehmiller Company, recognized he needed to make reforms at his manufacturing plants. He abolished the break bell to let workers take breaks when needed. He committed the company to paying market rates for every position. And in the midst of the Great Recession, he cut his salary to $10,000 and led the company in streamlining measures that protected every employee's job. At Building Bridges Professional Services in Grand Rapids, Michigan, Justin Beene hires high-risk young men from distressed urban neighborhoods. He has integrated more than 150 hours of life skills training each year as part of their paid employment. In Raleigh-Durham, North Carolina, Wendy Clark stretches the paychecks of her employees at Carpe Diem Cleaners by providing monthly vouchers worth a week of free groceries. In a small town west of Houston, Texas, Yvonne Streight has created dignified employment for over 200 individuals with disabilities at Brookwood Community.

CONSUMMATION

Jesus' life on earth inaugurated this work of renewal, but it did not complete it. Jesus has pledged to return to finish the job. The big story's fourth chapter has yet to unfold. But "the life of the world to the come" (for which the Nicene Creed tells us to look) has, in some senses, already arrived. The kingdom is both now and not yet.

This truth should nurture within us both a sense of bold optimism and a sense of quiet realism. Much change is possible now through the resurrection power of Jesus. In Huntsville, Alabama, Christians from several congregations have been deploying their particular vocational gifts as lawyers, educators, scientists, real estate developers, and healthcare workers alongside the residents of Lincoln Mill Village. In just over a decade, they've turned the local elementary school from the "red zone" (dangerously low test scores) to a shining academic success story, rehabbed almost 20 homes, and started a preschool. Crime and drug activity in the neighborhood are noticeably down.

But Christians are not utopians because we know the fully con-summated kingdom will only come with Christ's return. Our task is to work now with what pastor Tom Nelson calls "hopeful realism." We strive for the redemptive edge of our vocations, resisting evil and promoting good. Architect Jill Kurtz not only designs "green" buildings, she's teaching future generations of architects at Kansas State to consider creative ways they can make their talents accessi-ble and affordable to nonprofits who need them. Interior designer Cynthia Leibrock has learned the principles of "universal design" and is using them to create living spaces that enhance the mobility and dignity of people with physical handicaps. Back in the 1960s, insurance agent Bruce Copeland was motivated by his faith to labor faithfully for years to promote the rights of women and minorities at the Philadelphia-based firm. Today, entrepreneur Kelly Burton has launched Founders of Color because research shows that Black and Latino-owned companies grow at a slower pace than White-owned firms. Her platform offers minority-led firms access to relevant infor-mation, data, and the relationships and opportunities they need to scale quickly. These "hopeful realists" are thinking outside the box, taking risks, and refusing to simply "do things the way they've always been done." But they also are humble, recognizing that institutional change takes a long time and requires the Spirit's supernatural power.

In the midst of it all, though, our hearts burn for the New City. The consummation chapter of the big story tells us the glorious happy end-ing. Heaven and earth will be one. Shalom in its fullest will one day again reign. All will be set right. Evil, death, suffering, and injustice will all be destroyed.

The numerous Old Testament previews of the coming new heav-ens and new earth (Is 65:17-25; Zech 8:3-5; Ezek 34:25-31; Ps 72; Amos 9:11-15) offer us glimpses into what life in the age to come will be like. These passages depict something far different than the insipid, mud-dle-headed pictures of our culture's notions of "heaven." The New Jerusalem is teeming with life and culture. We see gardens, trees, cities, music, architecture, feasting — not disembodied souls flitting about clouds playing harps.

Admittedly, the Bible tells us the least about chapter four of the story. There's much we don't know. But it's clear that the hope of heaven is physical: We're looking (again in the exhortation of the Nicene Creed) for the resurrection of our bodies and the life of a world to come. We're looking forward to feasting and ruling. We're looking forward to life in a just and righteous community of beautiful diversity.

And what we're looking for then should inform how we're living now. The consummation chapter tells us that Jesus will return to earth proclaiming, "Behold, I am making all things new (Rev 21:5) — not "I am making all new things." The final chapter is not about God throwing this world in the trash and starting over. It is about God refining all things, burning away everything in his creation that became anti-shalom because of evil and sin.

Because human culture and civilization is going to endure into the next life, Andy Crouch suggests we ask ourselves this question: "How might my work in this vocational sector be furnishing the New Jerusalem?"

In light of where all redemptive history is going; in light of the reality that heaven is coming down to earth; in light of orthodox Christian teaching that tells us there is more to the story than just our souls being saved, our work today matters and may have eternal significance beyond what we can imagine.

———

Amy L. Sherman is a senior fellow at the Sagamore Institute and author of Kingdom Calling: Vocational Stewardship for the Common Good. *Sherman lives in Charlottesville, Virginia.*

God's Mission:
An Invitation to Participate in the Redemption of Individuals and Renewal of All Things

MICHAEL W. GOHEEN

When we speak of God's mission what are we talking about? The word "mission" is not found in Scripture. But like the words "Trinity" and "providence," it is a theological word that seeks to capture the teaching of Scripture. Where, then, do we go to grasp how the word might be used theologically to encapsulate the Bible's teaching? We might go to the etymology of the word, which is the Latin word mittere (to send) and look for the meaning in the sending action of God, which includes also the sending of the church. Or we might trace the language of God's mission back to 20th century discussions of mission theology where the word first arose to challenge a human-centered approach to the church's mission. No doubt both would be helpful. But a theology that is faithful will be contextual, and the question we face today is how most people would understand that word.

So, perhaps there is another place to start: One prominent way the word "mission" is used today in our culture is a "mission-statement." This is a well-known phenomenon. Business Dictionary defines a mission statement as "A written declaration of an organization's core purpose and focus that normally remains unchanged over time. ... a mission is something to be accomplished ..." And this is a good place to start to understand God's mission in Scripture. As we read the biblical story, the questions include "What is God's purpose? What is the focus of his activity that remains constant throughout the biblical narrative? What is God trying to accomplish?"

Paul tells us God has a plan and he is working it out in history. His plan has an ultimate goal he is moving toward, a purpose he has willed for the creation (Eph 1:11). What is that purpose? The Bible describes this in many different ways. For example, Paul says the goal is to reconcile to himself all things, whether things on earth or in heaven (Col 1:20). Peter describes this goal as the restoration of everything as promised by the prophets (Acts 3:21). Jesus tells us the purpose of God's mission is the renewal of all things (Matt 19:28).

There is another image given to us in the first book of the Bible. The purpose that God has for all of creation is blessing. The blessing that was enjoyed in the original creation, both by the non-human creation (Gen 1:22) and in human life (Gen 1:28), will be restored first to his chosen people and then through them to the whole world (Gen 12:2-3; Gal 3:8-9).

In many Christian traditions the word "blessing" has been emptied of its rich biblical content, so it's important to pause and reflect on its meaning here. It refers to God's purpose for humankind to thrive and flourish, to find unhindered delight and deep satisfaction as our needs are fully met in the abundance of creation and ultimately in God himself. It is always relational: Blessing can only be experienced in communion with God and with others. This is the marvelous purpose God has for humankind.

Reconciliation, restoration, renewal, blessing — all of these images point to how God's mission is to restore creation and humankind to flourish again as he designed it in the beginning. The goal of God's mission is not to take individual people from the world to live spiritually in heaven, but to restore people to live the fullness of bodily human lives on the restored creation according to God's original created design. The goal of God's mission is a comprehensive restoration of the world.

This means we must understand what the creation was supposed to be, why it is not that way, and how God is restoring the world to its original purpose.

BLESSING: THE WAY THE CREATION WAS SUPPOSED TO BE

The first few chapters of Scripture are foundational for the rest of the biblical story. It describes the creation as it was supposed to be, and that description functions in the rest of the Bible as the backdrop of God's work of restoration. The unfolding story is to return creation to what it was meant to be. In these first chapters we see that human beings were made to live in four relationships: to God, to each other in a variety of relationships, to creation, and to themselves. And there was shalom — a harmonious symphony of delight. There was shalom with God as they served, loved, and worshiped him. There was shalom among humanity as each served the other in selfless love. There was shalom with the non-human creation as human beings protected and cared for it. There was shalom experienced by each person as all

The goal of God's mission is a *comprehensive restoration of the world*.

created aspects[4] found their rightful place in a harmonious coherence centered in and directed to the service of God and the other. Creation was like a symphony where each instrument and sound found its place within the harmony of the whole. And it was very good.

The first words human beings hear from God are to rule and subdue the creation (Gen 1:26-28), explained further to develop the potential of the creation while caring for it (Gen 2:15). This has been often referred to as the cultural or creation mandate. Some have disputed whether it is a mandate at all and say that it is God's blessing pronounced over humankind.[5] In either case, humanity is blessed with the vocation of exploring and discovering all the rich and delightful potential in the creation for their own delight and benefit, for the glory of God, for love of their fellow human being, and for the good of the creation. Thus, humanity is made to work in community, and it is very good.

Central to this original vocation is stewardship.[6] Stewardship involves three things: being entrusted with resources to administer, a task to carry out, and accountability. Humanity has been entrusted with creation and each person has been given certain gifts to take part in developing and caring for it. Each one is tasked to serve God and faithfully reflect him in their calling so the culture we create together is a theatre of his glory. Moreover, we are to love one another in the context of community by faithfully employing our unique gifts to provide useful goods and services that meet the needs of our neighbor. And finally, we are to accomplish our task in loving the non-human creation as we develop the potential God has hidden in each part of it. And we are held accountable: This creation belongs to God and we will one day give account for how we exercised our gifts and used God's resources. Have we loved our neighbor or served ourselves? Have we served God or and idol? Have we cared for or exploited the creation?

As humanity carries out their vocation, there is a historical unfolding of creation. The biblical story begins in a garden and ends in a city, and this kind of development is built into the structure and meaning of creation. A city — a place where human beings live together in a variety of enriching relationships, meeting one another's needs in reciprocal love, and together stamping God's image on the world — this was God's intention.

CURSE OF SIN DESTROYS BLESSING: NOT THE WAY IT'S SUPPOSED TO BE

This glorious plan was destroyed by the act of human rebellion (Gen 3:1-7). Instead of living as God intended, human beings refused their allegiance and chose to listen to another word from the pit of hell. This act of rebellion wasn't simply an isolated act of disobedience that could be undone by a *mea culpa* and reversing course. This was a momentous act of treason that opened the floodgates to every kind of evil and misery that we see in the world today. Everything in creation was befouled and polluted by this original act of disobedience.

The relationship of God to humanity was broken. People were shut out from God's presence and cut off from the source of life (Gen 3:23-24). Human beings turned from serving each other's needs in selfless love to exploiting others in a self-serving pursuit (Gen 3:16). No longer was the work of their hands used to love others but utilized in destructive ways: The wonder of tool-making to fashion an instrument of murder and the beauty of human language and poetry to celebrate it (Gen 4:22-24). Creation itself now groans beneath a curse (Gen 3:17-19; Rom 8:19-22). Care for the creation was replaced by exploitation and selfish mastery. Life in the creation was difficult and would ultimately lead to death (Gen 3:17-19). The original symphony of created life was replaced by a discordant cacophony of idols that replaced God as the core that harmonized the parts.

The early chapters of the Bible unfold the ominous crescendo and the escalating consequences of sin. Curse replaces blessing.[7] And it is when we see the climax — or better the nadir — of the whole account in the story of the Tower of Babel (Gen 11:1-9) that we understand the nature of sin. We often view sin as individual acts of disobedience, and certainly that is included. But the Old Testament leads the way in seeing human rebellion in terms of idolatry: "all sin is an expression of the basic sin of idolatry, of putting something else in the place of God."[8] God's plan for humanity has gone wrong. Babel is a picture of the wrong kind of city, a city shaped by idolatry.

Paul offers a description of the way sin works (Rom 1:18-32). Human beings are made to serve God, but they often find another god within creation to orient their lives around. And since humanity always lives in community, forming a society and culture together, their idolatry will always take this form. They fashion their gods, create a society and culture in the image of those gods, and those gods, in turn, shape human beings more and more in their image.[9] Paul describes in typical Old Testament and Jewish fashion the way of sin in the world. Humanity serves together the creature rather than the Creator (Rom 1:21-23), and God gives them over to their idolatry (Rom 1:24, 26, 28), leading to a culture that is unjust, immoral, and where the image of God has unraveled (Rom 1:28-32).

Thus, each aspect of cultural life — leisure, work, economic, political, educational, technological, artistic, and so on — now finds its place in the idolatrous patterns shaped by serving idols rather than the living God. The New Testament calls this the world (Rom 12:2; James 4:4).

RESTORATION OF BLESSING: RETURNING THE WORLD TO THE WAY IT'S SUPPOSED TO BE

The story of the Bible is one of recovery — recovering God's original purpose and design for his whole creation. God's mission is to restore his whole creation (Acts 3:21), to reconcile all things back to its original shalom and harmony (Col 1:20) and renew the world to what it was supposed to be (Matt 19:28). God's mission is restoration — regaining what was corrupted. And it is comprehensive — every aspect of creation will one day be healed to again find its place in God's creational symphony.

Comprehensive restoration — this is the goal of God's mission. The Bible tells us the story of how he gets there. God's mission is successively carried out through Israel's mission, Jesus' mission, and the church's mission.

Israel's Mission

God's mission runs first of all through the nation of Israel. It will be this nation that is the means by which God will deal with the curse of sin in the world. They are chosen to bear in their life the promise of God's purpose of blessing for the sake of all. Israel will become the nucleus of restored humankind that will again enjoy the blessing of creation. The nations would be incorporated into this community and also experience this blessing.

This is the promise given to Abraham at the key juncture of God's mission. God says to Abraham that he will make him into a great nation and will restore the blessing of creation to him. But he will be blessed so that blessing might also go to all nations (Gen 12:2-3). It would be as Abraham's descendants follow the ways of the Lord by doing what is right and just that they will embody God's blessing and bear this promise for all creation (Gen 18:18-19). This is given in further detail in Exodus. When Israel is redeemed from the gods of Egypt, they are called to play a priestly role amidst the nations, and they are to mediate God's creational blessing to all peoples (Exod 19:3-6).

The Torah is given to guide the lives of God's people. The Torah is rooted in creation and offers a contextual implementation of what God intends for human life. The law is human cultural life centered in God rather than idols. If Israel would live by this law on the land, they would live out the righteousness, justice, mercy, and love God intended for human life (Deut 4:6-8). In short, Israel was called to embody blessing, what God intended in the beginning for human life. The Torah covered all of life — economics, work, politics, agriculture, family, and so on. Israel was to be the nucleus of a restored humanity that embodied God's creational intention. Thus, N. T. Wright can say that Israel's mission was to "model genuinely human existence"[10] so "the nations will see in Israel what it means to be truly human."[11]

Israel fails to model genuinely human existence and instead, like the other nations, turns to idols. God punished and exiled them from the land. But God sends prophets, and they have a message of hope. God will gather Israel and restore them to their calling. He will give them new hearts and the Spirit that they might truly live as the new humanity (Ezek 36:24-28). God will re-establish a nucleus of the restored humankind in the midst of the world as a rallying point for all nations. The other nations will be incorporated into this new humanity (Is 2:2-5). The entire creation will be included in God's ultimate renewing work (Is 65:17-25). God will restore the creation and the whole of human life to what it was meant to be.

This work of renewal, according to the prophets, would be the work of a Messiah, a Son of David, who would usher in a worldwide and everlasting kingdom (2 Sam 7:11-16; Ezek 37:24-28). God would carry out his end-time renewing work through this king by the powerful working of his Spirit (Joel 2:28; Is 61:1-11).

And so, Israel waited for God to carry out this work.

Christ's Mission

Israel failed in their mission, but God promised he would not leave it that way. The way of God's mission runs next through Jesus the Christ. Jesus fulfills the mission God gave to Israel as he deals with sin and its curse once and for all. Jesus also fulfills Israel's mission to embody God's purpose of blessing and invite others into it.

We might summarize the mission of Jesus with three words: revelation, accomplishment, and presence. Jesus reveals the blessing God intends for the creation. In his life Jesus launches an all-out assault on every form of evil: sickness, demon-possession, personal sin, economic, political, and social injustice, religious self-righteousness, and more. If God's power is present to attack sin and its effects, then the kingdom has come (Matt 11:1-6; 12:28). Jesus accomplishes the blessing that God intends for his world in his death and resurrection. In his death he takes on himself sin, demonic power, and cultural idolatry and defeats it once and for all (Col 2:15). In his resurrection he inaugurates his new creation where the powers at work in his ministry are now available in foretaste to his people by the Spirit (1 Pet 1:3-5; Acts 2:17). God's people are now able to experience in foretaste the life of blessing God has purposed for the creation.

Throughout his life a primary focus of Jesus' ministry is to gather the lost sheep of Israel (Matt 15:24) and restore them to their true vocation (Matt 5-7).[12] The Gospel accounts end with a sending: Gathered and restored Israel is sent to make known God's purpose of blessing in the midst of all nations. All peoples are to be gathered into this starting point of the new humankind.

Church's Mission

Jesus gathers Israel and restores them to their calling. Now their calling is transformed. Now they are a witness in their lives, words, and deeds to the victory that Jesus won over sin. They no longer bear the promise of blessing as only something in the future but embody now the first fruits and preview of the blessing that will one day fill the earth.

But the form of God's people changes, and this has huge ramifications. They are no longer just an ethnic and geographical people who live together as a cultural community shaped by the Torah. Now God's people are a multiethnic and non-geographical people and must find ways to live out the whole of their lives within cultures where other gods reign and give unity to life, within societies where idolatry resides structurally.

This means the witness of God's people to the blessing he intends for cultural life will involve a missionary encounter. As the church embodies God's creational intention in all of public life there is the need for discernment that distinguishes between the creational

Now God's people
and non-
people and must
live out the
lives within
other gods reign
to life, within
idolatry resides

are a multiethnic
geographical
find ways to
whole of their
cultures where
and give unity
societies where
structurally.

MICHAEL W. GOHEEN

insight reflected in cultural patterns as well as the idolatry that twists it. God's people must not be conformed to the world but offer new patterns of blessing as a preview of what will one day fill the earth (Rom 12:1-2).

THE COMPLETION OF GOD'S MISSION AND OUR MISSION TODAY

Jesus promises the work he began will come to completion when he returns. Then sin and all its effects will be removed from the creation. The purpose to restore the blessing of his original design will be complete. The creation will be restored to its original blessing once and for all. There will be a glorious renewal of life on earth when we shall be more fully human than we ever have been. We will be liberated from the idolatry and sin that binds and dehumanizes us. The shalom of all of human life and every part of creation will be restored.

Until that day we have been given a foretaste of this blessing by the Spirit. A foretaste is an actual taste of the food with the promise that the full meal is coming. Until that full blessing arrives, we are a preview of the coming blessing of the kingdom. A movie preview is actual footage of the movie designed to interest the viewer in the future attraction. The church is to be a preview of the harmony, the selfless love of others, the service of God, and care for the creation that will one day fill the earth.

What might it look like today to be a community that lives as a preview of this blessing in our vocational and economic lives?

- A community of contentment, simplicity, and generosity in a world of insatiable desire, greed, and envy;
- A community of patience and self-control in a world of instant gratification;
- A community of joy and thankfulness in a world of dissatisfaction;
- A community of mutual accountability in a world of individual autonomy;

- A community of self-giving love and sacrificial service in a world of selfish ambition;
- A community of stewardship in a world of waste;
- A community of justice in a world of economic and ecological injustice;
- A community whose commitment to Christ includes public life in a world where religion is considered private;
- A community willing to suffer in its encounter with idolatry in a world that seeks comfort and ease;
- A community that loved and blessed all those who stood in opposition to the gospel;
- A community of peace-makers in the midst of a world of conflict increasingly divided by idolatrous ideology;
- A community that refuses the economic and political options of the left and right in a world where those seem to be the only way;
- A community whose lives were oriented to the poor and marginalized in a world that panders to the rich and powerful;
- A community of integrity of character in a world of surface image designed for self- promotion;
- A community of steady faithfulness in a world with a short attention span that pursues the next best thing;
- A community that acknowledges God's normative order in a world obsessed with human autonomy;
- A community that makes economic choices based on what is best for the poor and the environment rather than on what makes the greatest profit; and
- A community that spent itself on useful products and services in a world that orients administration of economic goods to those who can afford more.

A community that lives like this would offer a preview of blessing to a world that needs to see a way beyond the idolatry that is destroying us. And it would be attractive! But most of all God's name would be honored as we demonstrated what it would mean to be fully human.

———

Michael Goheen is theological director of the Missional Training Center in Phoenix, Arizona, and professor of missional theology at Covenant Theological Seminary, St. Louis, Missouri. Goheen and his wife, Marnie, split their time between Phoenix and Surrey, British Columbia.

Personal Wholeness:
Vital for Effective Leadership

GARY BLACK, JR.

In recent years a good number of non-profit Christian institutions and foundations have focused their attention on the moral foundations of prosperity and the necessary ethical foundations required for a society to flourish. These groups are engaging in crucial work to assist us in reimagining our previous conceptions and assumptions of complicated religious, economic, political, and social issues.[13] Some of these organizations have realized that to best understand what factors lead to developing and sustaining, a holistically flourishing life, a society must also hold a robust understanding of what is good and right. In short, to live a "good" life, one must first understand and properly define what is, and is not, good.

It is instructive to recognize that ancient philosophers and theologians were aware and devoted time to pursuing credible answers to what is good. Classic philosophy and religion tend to focus on seeking answers to four basic questions, beginning with "What is the good life?" The great thinkers of every era have settled on the inescapable truth that human beings continually search for the components they

Can we *build good buildings* without using good bricks?

believe will provide them a good life. To begin to answer this, one must also come to understand what is good, and also is real or lasting, which are the second and third questions. Finally, one must seek to understand the processes required to answer the final question: How does one become a good person? All these components must converge to establish a foundation for human wholeness and flourishing.

Despite all that has changed across human history, the necessity of coming to reliable answers for these four questions has not changed. Ironically, what our increasingly secular, post-modern, post-Christian society is coming to re-realize is that economic, political, and social systems that affect huge swaths of our lives are themselves, like it or not, inherently moral realities. Ancient writers and thinkers like Plato, Aristotle, Cicero, Augustine, and Aquinas intrinsically knew that our social systems cannot succeed in creating the means to achieve human wholeness and thriving unless they incorporate and apply basic moral values. We must maintain a vivid understanding of what is good and bad, right and wrong, true and false in order to live good lives.

The Bible manifests unwavering support for the necessity of moral goodness within our economic, social, religious, and political responsibilities. This is most often referred to in Scripture as stewardship. The ancient Greek word for this stewardship task is oikonomos. Two important concepts are conveyed in the Greek understanding of a steward's role. The first concept is revealed by the prefix oiko (oy-coe), which is often translated home, house, dwelling place, or habitat. The second word nomos (no-moose) can mean rules, law, or custom. Therefore, the notion of oikonomos carries the idea of one who manages or applies the rules for a house. Today we might use the term leader, manager, overseer, or boss for those who occupy these types of oikonomos roles. Thus, a Christian disciple is expected to steward themselves and their work for the glory of God, God's kingdom objectives, for the benefit of everyone involved. This is commonly understood today as a fiduciary (faith or trust filled) relationship.[14]

The question I want to consider in this essay is whether and to what degree the holistic moral wellness of leaders, the people-in-charge, is crucial to every societal endeavor. Can we have good societies without good leaders? Can we have good societies or institutions if they are not stewarded by morally sound leaders who seek to both know and then do good for all concerned? Put another way, "Can we build good buildings without using good bricks?" Today it seems clear that some believe any brick, no matter how unstable, will do.

Several years ago, while in the waiting room of my doctor's office I remember finding a then article in *Forbes Magazine* written by Karl Moore.[15] Moore is a professor on the Desautels Faculty at McGill University and was an associate fellow at Green Templeton College at Oxford University. He has spent much of his career reading, writing, and teaching about leadership. The article in my hands was Moore's short review of Barbara Kellerman's book, The End of Leadership.[16] Kellerman is the founding director of Harvard's Kennedy School Center for Public Leadership. Early in the article Moore made this significant point:

> The current culture has emboldened followers, as Kellerman says, to "feel entitled to pry into their leaders' lives – and to hold them accountable for what they do." There has been a strong diminishment of authority in American culture. The ease of informa-

tion dissemination, mainly through advancement in
technology, had sped this devolution of power, as
most can not only gain information more quickly, but
can also discuss it with one another openly on the
web. The impact of WikiLeaks for instance, was to
diminish and expose leaders of American politics as
being inept, weak and at times corrupt. Once this type
of information starts to flow, it is very difficult to put it
back in the box. This in turn, leads to a perception that
leaders no longer merit their authority.[17]

After finishing the article, I thought about how Moore and Kellerman's insights might apply to both my experience in Christian organizations, and more broadly, to American culture as a whole. Do we
even care to know the truth? Does it matter to us if our leaders are eth-
ically moral people or are we simply entertained by their fall? Have we
come to the point where a certain level of effectiveness in a leadership
role is the only real measurement of success? Do our leaders have any
responsibility to those they lead to be an example of moral courage and
integrity? If we probe this line of questioning more deeply, we could
even ask if a leader has a moral responsibility to steward his or her own
soul well before God? If so, how are they to do that?

At a meta-level, part of our problem may be found in American or
Western versions of evangelical Christianity. Our evangelical institutions (churches, universities, seminaries, parachurch organizations, etc.) have, for some time now, largely overlooked the subject
of personal, moral character formation. We, and many of our most
"successful" institutions have tended to focus on evangelism, and/or
numerical/financial growth, to the detriment of robust discipleship.
(See footnote for a more complete definition of discipleship.)[18] There
are many reasons for this that require more intensive attention than
can be done here.[19] However, one key motivation for this lack of attention to discipleship is imbedded in a misapplication of a key biblical doctrine. When the theological tenets of justification by faith are

thought to be the beginning and end of the gospel story, then sanctification becomes a non-essential add on to the Christian life. A biblically valid understanding and application of Christlike discipleship, and the habits of sin it seeks to address and transform, is becoming progressively lost to mainstream evangelical congregations, universities, and seminaries. Sin, it turns out, doesn't preach very well to a consumer driven society. In sum, Christian discipleship demands surrendering to the process of holistic transformation of character as an inescapable priority of the gospel Jesus preached. In this way the gospel is how Jesus provides for human beings to experience the unbridled wholeness God originally intended for us to experience and share.

Many Christian organizations will undoubtedly argue they have great numbers of programs and activities under the auspices of "discipleship ministries." Yet, again, measuring actual results is much more important than simply creating activities with religiously acceptable marketing labels. The closest one may get to a biblical understanding of discipleship in our contemporary churches today is most likely to be found in some form of recovery ministry. Addicts, those recovering from divorce or abuse, or those related to, and therefore suffering from the accompanying consequences of these decisions, will often have a practical understanding of the effects of sin and the necessity for character transformation. Unfortunately, these "recovery" ministries, though vital to the cause of Christ, tend to be outside the core purposes and vision of most churches. Hence too many modern Christians still tend to consider the prospect of discipleship as a non-essential aspect of Christian faith. Today many Christians treat spiritual transformation like the "protective" undercoating often presented to new car buyers as a luxury item; it has little or nothing to do with why they were attracted to the car in the first place.

In discipleship's place we now talk about belonging to a community or a small group of some sort. All of which may be fine and good, if these groups are prepared and devoted to provide the level of intention the New Testament routinely demonstrates is necessary for engaging the types of personal and relational issues involved in moral character formation. In my experience this is rarely the case and often not the intention that tends to draw these kinds of groups together. Social groups that spend time in Bible study and prayer are important. But the evidence suggests that these types of fellowships alone are not developing the degree of moral character formation our society so desperately requires. Congregational leaders must train effective disciples, not just small group facilitators. Moral character is not formed by osmosis any more than it is developed through discussion groups led by well-meaning yet untrained leaders who are given no greater objective other than to make people feel welcome in order to generate faithful attendance. These are not the same intentions we find highlighted in the pages of the New Testament.

I propose it is the lack of a defined and applied process for moral formation, combined with a resistance to measure the success or failures of our current discipleship programs within our Christian institutions, that are the main causes behind the collapse of moral leadership that Moore and Kellerman describe. I fear the collapse of moral integrity and ethical leadership has now risen to epidemic proportions in the contemporary society and threatens to become the new normal. The recent #MeToo movement, which has spilled into our Christian organizations, is a case in point.[20] We must know why and how to stem this tide.

Furthermore, I suggest that leaders do have a moral responsibility to themselves, to God, and to those they serve through their leadership capacity, to steward their private and public lives in a godly way. I also propose that until our Christian leaders, both laity and clergy, advocate for, and personally engage in, a transparent and holistic process of moral character formation, our churches will not follow suit. It must begin and be sustained at the highest leadership positions in our organizations or it won't happen at all. Leaders lead best when they guide others to places they have visited themselves.

It is my firm belief that this level of moral stewardship of the body of Christ can and must take place. This is more than a blind hope or wishful thinking. We are fortunate that the process of moral character formation is simple to understand and apply. Everyone, regardless of place or position, can start wherever they find themselves, at any moment, to become an ever more faithful disciple of the life and teachings of Jesus. The first requirement is to decide one wants to follow in the footsteps of Christ. That the decision is simple and easy to understand does not mean the path is easy. However, we do have some good guides to encourage and help us along the way.

RENOVATION OF THE HEART

Some of the best thinking and writing on the subject of the good life and the process of moral character development comes to us through the insights and lived example of philosopher and theologian Dallas Willard. Willard's understanding of the human person is crucial to our task of holistic, transformational character development in our leaders. This can be found in his important yet widely overlooked work Renovation of the Heart.[21]

As a brief overview of Willard's project, Renovation of the Heart starts with an insightful investigation of the human self. His under-

I fear the collapse of moral integrity and ethical leadership has now risen to epidemic proportions in the contemporary society and *threatens to become the new normal.*

standing of the best practices available for the transformation of moral character is best highlighted in what he calls the "Circles of the Self." He then expands this analysis by conjoining Jesus' gospel announcement of the reality of God's kingdom as the same means of grace that must also capture and transform each arena of a person's life; first the heart/spirit/will, then the mind, followed by the body, all of which then proceeds into each of our personal relationships. As this progressive transformation occurs, one's entire soul, or life, is increasingly redeemed or sanctified more fully into the likeness of the character of Christ.

Willard took great pains to define and describe all the key areas of a person's life that must come under the guidance and grace of God in order to experience lasting flourishing. The "Circles of the Self" begin to unfold a much-needed, yet rarely understood, explanation of the multi-layered, interdependent, symbiosis involved in the individual parts of everyday life. Willard argues that the overarching goal for any follower of Christ is to develop a level of integrity of character that allows one to take on the easy yoke of Jesus and results in applying the greatest commandment in every aspect of our lives (Matt 22:35-40).

Over the years many readers have found Willard's descriptions and warnings regarding the nature of the "ruined" (sin focused) soul a hauntingly accurate reflection of their own spiritual condition. But he did not leave the reader hopeless. Willard takes great pains to meticulously describe how each of the intricate aspects of the human self can come under the love, grace, and freedom provided for those who abide in "the way, the truth and the life" of Christ. Many leaders have found Willard's insights invaluable when seeking the intentions (why) and means (how) for establishing a careful, thoughtful, transformational, lifelong pursuit of Christlike character. Willard argues that such a life of abundance, modeled after Christ, is not only possible, but has been attained by many dedicated disciples over the ages. Renovation also specifically points to how and why Jesus in particular can and must be considered Christianity's primary teacher and guide for Christian living. This is an idea too often forgotten today even in some of our most outwardly Christian institutions. Jesus is brilliant. And this brilliance includes the best knowledge available of what moral character is and how it should be formed.

Finally, in discussing the how and why of individual spiritual formation and the transformation of the internal life, Willard investigates the need for both sustained effort on the part of the disciple combined with the sustaining grace of God. Here we find a robust description of what holistic transformation would look like in the life of a disciple, and in the world at large. Willard also goes on to describe how churches and their leaders can and must facilitate a curriculum of transformation and suggests some methods needed in order to assist such a change.

In short, Willard argued that everyone has both the potential and the obligation before God to tend to the realities of their own soul. In that regard we are all equal. However, Willard also taught that leaders carry a greater burden. Biblical leaderships involves accepting a higher responsibility to set an example of the means necessary for experiencing life to the full as a disciple of Jesus inside the kingdom of God.

The never-ending media barrage reveals leaders in nearly every area of our society, including Christian organizations, who are routinely discovered as failing to live up to their ethical and/or legal responsibilities. We read how leaders succumbed to some form of passion, a yearning, a weakness, a wound, an inappropriate relationship, and/or an ambition. The result is often a full-blown crisis that can threaten both the leaders and countless others at the existential level of the soul itself. Lifetimes of devotion are ruined, careers ended, institutions wrecked, marriages dissolved, trust destroyed, wounds inflicted, abuse of power runs amok in desperate attempts to hide the reality of it all, and worst of all, souls are set adrift. Too often the consequences of these failures carry lifetime sentences. Fortunately, nothing is beyond the mercy and forgiveness of Christ. But too few take the opportunity to abide in God's grace before they experience a moral failure. However, these failures also demonstrate that Willard's assessment and corrective is crucial for us to consider.

WASHING THE INSIDE OF THE CUP FIRST

Fortunately, we have a means of avoiding these calamities. Jesus helps us understand the importance of tending first to the heart, which is the wellspring of our lives (Prov 4:23). For many of us, this truth hits us too late in life. Jesus makes this point in Matthew 23:25-28 when he conveys some harsh truths to the religious leaders of his day:

> Woe to you, scribes and Pharisees, hypocrites! For you clean the outside of the cup and of the dish, but inside they are full of robbery and self-indulgence. You blind Pharisee, first clean the inside of the cup and of the dish, so that the outside of it may become clean also. Woe to you, scribes and Pharisees, hypocrites! For you are like whitewashed tombs which on the outside appear beautiful, but inside they are full of dead men's bones and all uncleanness. So you, too, outwardly appear righteous to men, but inwardly you are full of hypocrisy and lawlessness.

How do we escape the plight of the religious Pharisee who is only interested in religion as a means of behavior modification but is not devoted to the inward transformation of a hardened heart? What follows are suggestions for leaders interested in developing an enduring Christlike character that produces fruit of the Spirit.

LONG-TERM HABITS OF SELF-REFLECTION

To begin the process of developing the kind of holistic integrity required of leaders in every area of the kingdom of God, we must start with committing lengthy periods of time for consistent, deep, honest, inward self-reflection. This reflection must tap into, among other things, the current condition of every aspect of one's soul (heart/will, mind, body, and relationships) before God. There are several excellent examples to follow for how one can engage in this process. Two of which can be found on a short list of Christianity's classic heroes of the faith. Leaders interested in developing their moral courage and integrity would do well to dive headlong into the works of Teresa of Avila, especially her *The Interior Castle*, and Augustine's *Confessions*. These works demonstrate many great attributes and potentialities that can grow out of initiating a contemplative life.

Few of our leaders take the time or realize the importance of engaging in an ongoing moral inventory of their actions, attitudes, motives, goals, intentions, relationships, and the means they are employing to achieve their objectives. Yet this is precisely the level of gritty honesty we encounter in Teresa and Augustine's work. One helpful tool to begin the self-assessment process is from Discipleship Dynamics, an organization created by a Christian psychologist and seminary professor who saw the need for a robust, comprehensive, statistically valid means for providing meaningful feedback to those seeking spiritual growth and identifying strengths and areas for improvement. Utilizing 175 probing questions, the goal of the assessment tool is to provide a "biblical, whole-life discipleship assessment that measures growth in 5 Dimensions and 35 Outcomes, evaluating attitudes and actions."[22] Many find that using an assessment tool that offers some objective feedback can be a helpful way to quickly and easily jump start the introspective journey of contemplating the state of one's soul before God.

Secondly, once some data has been collected and a preliminary understanding of the status of one's soul has begun, leaders must then commit to developing robust, enduring friendships. This is a crucial and most undervalued step in a leader's internal life. The lack of development and commitment to faithful friendships is also where most efforts for moral transformation tend to flail and therefore fail. It is difficult to maintain one's devotion to the cause of Christ, much less the integrity of one's soul, without a true friend. Here the definition of "a friend" is key to understand. In his classic moral text, Nicomachean Ethics, the Greek philosopher Aristotle describes three kinds of friendships.[23] These are friends of pleasure, friends of utility, and friends of virtue. In short, friends of pleasure are those we seek to have a good time with. Friends of utility are often those we meet in the workplace, or who are our neighbors. We are friendly with these individuals in part because we need to work together for some purpose that necessitates a certain level of trustworthy relational interaction. Aristotle never suggests that friendships based on pleasure or utility are not important or valuable. They both serve important purposes in society.

THE IMPORTANCE OF VIRTUOUS FRIENDS

However, what neither a relationship based on pleasure or utility provide is an irreplaceable focus on what gives human life enduring meaning and transcendent purpose. For that, Aristotle realizes, we need friends of virtue, who are committed to us, and we to them, not because of what we will gain, or whether we will "have a good time" with them on Friday nights. Instead, friends of virtue are committed to us and we to them simply due to our shared commitment to the one another's highest and best good. These are the individuals who tell us the truth, and who we expect to tell us the truth, about the nature of who we are and what we are doing. They ask the hard questions, probe into our deepest hurts, and expose our most blinding lies. Friends of virtue are willing to push on sensitive areas of our lives and thus never shy away from the hard realities of life and leadership. Leaders can tend to be stubborn, prideful, overconfident in their own abilities and therefore blind to their faults. Leaders can also tend to listen only to either their fans or foes. Arrogant and insecure leaders are also well known for surrounding themselves with "yes" people, those who "get along by going along" with whatever the leader advises.

In contrast, friends of virtue try diligently to ground one another in reality. Therefore, they admonish and correct one another. Sometimes tough words and hard conversations are necessary. Some of the hardest words of encouragement come in the form of admonishment (Eph 4:11-16; 1 Tim 4; 2 Tim 2). There are moments where the temptation for a leader to save their job prevents them from doing their job. The propensity to rationalize excuses for shrinking in the face of adversity can be challenging. Friends of virtue help keep a leader's perspective and priorities in the appropriate places. This is often a messy and emotionally volatile hurdle for friends to navigate together. Yet maintaining some degree of false personal piety should never be used as an excuse to avoid the cluttered intricacies of the human condition. Too much is at stake. Friends of virtue walk headlong into the complexities of one another's souls out of a mutual love for, and understanding of, the power of virtue that enable us to live a life worthy of our calling.

Virtuous friendships are an indispensable necessity for any leader who hopes to live and lead in a way that honors the call of Christ. I would also suggest this is not a value I see celebrated in many of our churches. Living in community, unfortunately, is not often the same as living together as friends seeking virtue. Christian churches that seek to foster community for its own sake can tend to become devoted primarily to the benefits and pleasures of belonging to a certain group of likeminded people. In turn, those who carry differing perspectives or who challenge the status quo, even when unvirtuous or questionable activity is on display, can become demonized as dissenters with "divisive spirits." In contrast, Aristotelian friendships are singly devoted to the open display of righteous living and not a socially defined or contrived contract to experience "unity." The focus on Christlike character formation tends to be forgotten in communities where belonging becomes more important than becoming. For Christian leaders, having friends of virtue who are willing to pay the price for maintaining the priority of becoming more Christlike cannot be overemphasized.[24]

Of course, there are more spiritual disciplines and practices that will do wonders for character development. To name just a few, the discipline of secrecy carries great benefits for those in the public eye. For the more extroverted leader, the disciplines of solitude and silence are fundamental to best overcome the trappings of fame and self-importance. For those with more introverted personalities, perhaps the disciplines of fellowship and celebration may be a welcome means of coming out of a shell of isolation that many leaders struggle to escape. And there are many more. Still, the first steps in the process of developing a robust commitment to holistic wellness begins best, in my view, with first deciding personal moral character is not a luxury but a necessity that demands a keen level of devotion and commitment.

The appropriate disciplines are chosen and practiced after we have discovered where we need to grow. For instance, if a person is struggling to keep their opinions to themselves, or if a leader tends to be a bit overbearing and controlling, the disciplines of fasting and silence may be helpful in combating such tendencies. Or, if a leader has a tendency to be standoffish and isolated, the disciples of fellowship and celebration can often do wonders in helping to reconnect the leader to their team and establishing a sense of camaraderie. It is important to note that spiritual disciplines help us practice "off the spot" what character trait we desire to display when we are "on the spot." Just as athletes spend thousands of hours practicing hitting baseballs or shooting jump shots before the game ever begins, so too leaders must practice embodying the characteristics of godliness necessary for their callings as well. Finally, every leader, just like each athlete, will have some natural tendencies for success in some areas and struggles in others. What the disciplines provide is a means of discovering, then working to improve, areas of improvement long before they manifest in moments that count. Here again, good friends will commit to discussing, evaluating, and then developing strategies to address what the disciplines reveals.

A RULE OF LIFE

With a commitment to the disciplined life established, leaders must then resolve within themselves to focus on the areas of weakness in character or lack of maturity in their spiritual development. For some this might produce what historic Christians down through the ages have termed a Rule of Life.[25] Simply defined, a Rule of Life is a set of resolutions and commitments one makes that provide a structure and direction for growth in spiritual wholeness. A rule attempts to establish "a rhythm for life in which is helpful for being formed by the Spirit, a rhythm that reflects a love for God and respect for how he has made us."[26] Prayerfully developing a Rule of Life, in partnership with good friends, seeking the good life in God's kingdom together is an excellent way leaders can endeavor to follow the greatest commandment to love God with all one's heart, soul, mind, and strength, while seeking to love others as Christ has loved us.

Again, spiritual disciplines combined with a Rule of Life are a means only, not the end. The disciplines themselves are not a form of righteousness. One is not spiritually mature because they routinely engage the disciplines of fasting, solitude, silence, or giving. What is unfortunately often overlooked by Christian leaders is taking time to evaluate the effects the disciplines do or do not have on one's life. Like all disciplines, whether physical disciplines applied in athletics, playing musical instruments, or medical procedures, or when engaging mental disciplines applied to academic studies or writing, disciplined practices are intended to create an increasing degree of ease in the activity being engaged. One practices their musical scales in order to become better adept at playing music. Likewise, the effects of our spiritual disciplines in a Rule of Life need to be measured and adapted when necessary to attain full effect. One is not mature or righteous simply because spiritual disciplines are practiced. We often misplace our focus on what it is the disciplines are. They are tools, not guarantees or rewards — means of grace and not meritorious for salvation. True friends will help us keep these priorities in line and assist us in

A Rule of Life is a set of _resolutions and commitments_ one makes that provide a structure and direction for growth in spiritual wholeness.

tracking our progress as they journey with us and we with them. If these important steps are taken, good things tend to happen because God is not willing that any should perish.

In conclusion, I desperately want to find evidences in our Christian leaders to disprove Kellerman and Moore's thesis. I find myself often asking what if the media were given unlimited access to the lives of Christian leaders who have willingly submitted themselves to the rigors of moral character formation described in the New Testament as the discipleship program of Jesus? What would be the result? What if, under the microscope of scrutiny, the media found not perfect people, but authentically genuine, moral, courageous, altruistic, loving, merciful, and ruthlessly honest individuals who know and do good for those they serve? What kind of witness would that be to an increasingly cynical post-Christian society?

A tragic example of courageous moral leadership can be found in the midst of a horrific and recent sexual abuse scandal involving Larry Nassar. Olympic gymnast Rachael Denhollander was the first of many to file a police complaint against Nassar, her former doctor, for sexual assault when she was 15. It was later reported that Nassar may have been responsible for sexual crimes with over 150 women, many of which were minors.[27] In a courageously honest op-ed in The New York Times, Denhollander offered some perspective on the hardships she has faced as a result of her decision to expose Nassar and her willingness to advocate for other victims of his crimes:

> I lost my church. I lost my closest friends as a result of advocating for survivors who had been victimized by similar institutional failures in my own community. I lost every shred of privacy. When a new friend searched my name online or added me as a friend on Facebook, the most intimate details of my life became available long before we had even exchanged phone numbers. I avoided the grocery stores on some days, to make sure my children didn't see my face on the newspaper or a magazine. I was asked questions about things no one should know when I least wanted to talk. And the effort it took to move this case forward — especially as some called me an "ambulance chaser" just "looking for a payday" — often felt crushing.

> Yet all of it served as a reminder: These were the very cultural dynamics that had allowed Larry Nassar to remain in power. I knew that the farthest I could run from my abuser, and the people that let him prey on children for decades, was to choose the opposite of what that man, and his enablers, had become. To choose to find and speak the truth, no matter what it cost.[28]

At Nassar's sentencing hearing, Denhollander made this courageous statement:

The Bible you speak of carries a final judgment where all of God's wrath and eternal terror is poured out on men like you. Should you ever reach the point of truly facing what you have done, the guilt will be crushing. And that is what makes the gospel of Christ so sweet. Because it extends grace and hope and mercy where none should be found. And it will be there for you. I pray you experience the soul crushing weight of guilt, so you may someday experience true repentance and true forgiveness from God, which you need far more than forgiveness from me — though I extend that to you as well.

Throughout this process, I have clung to a quote by C.S. Lewis, where he says, my argument against God was that the universe seems so cruel and unjust. But how did I get this idea of just, unjust? A man does not call a line crooked unless he first has some idea of straight. What was I comparing the universe to when I called it unjust?

Larry, I can call what you did evil and wicked because it was. And I know it was evil and wicked because the straight line exists. The straight line is not measured based on your perception or anyone else's perception, and this means I can speak the truth about my abuse without minimization or mitigation. And I can call it evil because I know what goodness is. And this is why I pity you. Because when a person loses the ability to define good and evil, when they cannot define evil, they can no longer define and enjoy what is truly good.[29]

Unfortunately, too few of our contemporary Christian leaders today have accepted the call of moral leadership and character formation that Denhollander exemplifies. But what if we did? What if our leaders decided to engage in exactly the kind of moral inventory Denhollander describes and look into our own lives to discern what is crooked and what is strait? Then what if investigative teams did deep dive background checks into the lives of these disciples of Jesus and discovered real virtue instead of vice? What if the public was routinely confronted with widely published evidences of incontrovertible acts of moral courage, integrity, faithfulness, familial loyalty, graciousness, generosity, self-sacrifice, gentle patience, a fierce devotion to truth, a glowing respect for the intrinsic value of all persons, and a keen awareness of the differences between one's personal good and the common good? What if we had these same kinds of moral leaders in the fields of journalism that endeavored to put these kinds of credible testimonials before the public eye? Would leadership be dead then? Or would we be able to demonstrate once again how indefatigably necessary moral courage and visionary leadership is to our society? I argue the world is looking for and needs heroes today as much if not more than ever before. And the church should be full of heroes. It was once. There was a time the church was a hero factory. It must be again.

Our leaders must be held accountable. We must ask ourselves and our leaders, "Who are your friends of virtue? Who has the permission to ask you hard questions without fear of reprisal and has given you permission for the same? Who tracks your progress and comments on your regression? Who are you revealing the complexities of your soul to? Who knows about your secret successes and failures? Who have you let in? How are you intentionally seeking spiritual wholeness?" If we read these questions as good advice or interesting thoughts and yet cease to act, we become complacent. And the world continues to groan, waiting for the sons and daughter of God to be revealed. We, and they, deserve better. And God has provided exactly what we need to

Spiritual disciplines help us practice "off the spot" what character trait we desire to display when we are "on the spot."

GARY BLACK, JR.

live in the holistic flourishing and wholeness originally intended in the Garden. That reality still exists. And we don't have to die to experience it. Life from above is available now. In fact, Jesus stated it is "at hand," within our reach (Matt 3:2, 4:17). Glory to God.

"For the anxious longing of the creation waits eagerly for the revealing of the sons of God. For the creation was subjected to futility, not willingly, but because of Him who subjected it, in hope that the creation itself also will be set free from its slavery to corruption into the freedom of the glory of the children of God," (Rom 8:19-21).

———

Gary Black, Jr. is a professor of theology in the Azusa Pacific University Honors College and author of several books. He and Dallas Willard co-authored The Divine Conspiracy Continued. *Black lives in La Verne, California.*

The Goodness of Work:
Work That Leads to Flourishing

VINCENT BACOTE

I begin with a confession: Until recently, the proliferation of books, conferences and organizations focused on questions of faith, work, and economics has sometimes led me to believe the message was circling through a wide group of Christians. I had moments where I believed "most people are now hearing this great news about a faith that connects Sunday to all of the other days of the week." I learned this was a misguided, overly optimistic perspective. What opened my eyes? Among various factors that clarified this, two conversations I had at a recent faith, work, and economics conference revealed the need for the message to be spread more broadly and with more complexity.

TWO CONVERSATIONS

The first conversation occurred in a hallway outside of the venue for plenary sessions. A friend approached me with the concern that the event was a good one but not as good as it could be, particularly because the demographics of the event skewed largely white and male (including speakers and the authors of books sold at the event). His concern was that the lack of diversity in population and source materials might indicate these conferences were only relevant for a certain segment of the population; could it be that all the talk about the goodness of work was only for some and not others?

The second conversation occurred as a pastor friend drove me to the airport following the conference. He asked me about the relevance of all the language of the goodness and purpose of work for those who tend to regard their employment as jobs that put food on the table and pay the bills but not as a vocation or dimension of flourishing (flourishing is what happens once one is off from work in this view). If not a necessary evil, work is not much more than "what needs to be done." My pastor friend's question brought to mind one of the jobs I had when I was in college. I worked at a warehouse for two summers and over one holiday, and I vividly recall the juxtaposition between the physical labor required and the low level of intellectual engagement. While I liked working with some of the people and was glad to have a paycheck every two weeks, I sometimes said to myself "I would not want to do this kind of job for most of my life." At that time, and for those my friend had in mind, "goodness" and "work" did not share a clear connection. Would the people my pastor had in mind feel a dissonance at conferences connecting faith, work, and economics?

These two conversations reveal not only that the reach of the faith and work movement has been more limited than I assumed, but also an even greater challenge that is present for many Christians amid their work lives. The challenge is that in all kinds of denominations and local churches, the approaches to the formation of Christians is disconnected from work. This kind of formation of Christians is incomplete and makes it difficult to see the significance of matters often regarded as non-spiritual (such as all of the hours spent in the world of work), and hardly speaks to concerns connected to those whose work is "just a job" and to historical complications from race. Yet work is indeed good; the task of spiritual formation is incomplete without this important emphasis.

How do we move forward, considering both the questions raised at the conference and the need for Christian formation that emerges out of a more complete and coherent understanding of the drama revealed to us in God's Word? To answer this question, it is important to explore how the narrative of Scripture includes elements that help us see the ultimate goodness of work. Scripture also illuminates the way we address various challenges of diversity and workplace drudgery or lack of purpose.

Theological anthropology, our view of humanity, will help us move toward a better understanding of formation. In particular, this will provide a better perspective on work and a larger view of our participation in the mission God has given us.

While earlier chapters rehearsed the grand drama of Scripture, it is important to highlight the ways it reveals that goodness of work if we are to move forward. Incomplete approaches to formation often discuss the fall and redemption and set the stage for a faith that expresses salvation as a mode of escape from a world that is hopelessly sinful. To be fair, this is not surprising (at least in evangelical circles) in light of the way the gospel story is told as a kind of two stage model with sin and its implications as the first stage, and Christ's saving work as the resolution to this problem as the second stage. Moreover, the ways people continue to experience distress and disappointment can lead to the impression that our encounter with redemption is the solution (ultimately) for a world that fails to deliver "the good life" to us.

How does this connect to theological anthropology? There is an intimate connection between our doctrine of humanity and the four-act story of the Bible. In fact, it is impossible to talk about the story and not have at least an implicit theological anthropology, as questions of sin and salvation involve the human condition. The partial story that only emphasizes fall and redemption can lead us to a view of theological anthropology where the focus is mainly on the status of humans as estranged from God and in need of a savior to bring rescue, a new status, and final destination. The truncated view of humans leads to a dissonant or adversarial relationship between ideas not typically regarded as "spiritual." Elements of the four-act drama lead us to a more complete view of humanity and a better integrated view of Christian life, a different way of being "spiritual" persons.

THE FIRST GREAT COMMISSION

To begin with the doctrine of creation, the first act, we first learn that God intended to create humans with a tremendous purpose. Genesis 1:26-28[30] reads

> Then God said, "Let us make mankind in our image, in
> our likeness, so that they may rule over the fish in the
> sea and the birds in the sky, over the livestock and all
> the wild animals, and over all the creatures that move
> along the ground."
>
> So God created mankind in his own image,
> in the image of God he created them;
> male and female he created them.
>
> God blessed them and said to them, "Be fruitful and
> increase in number; fill the earth and subdue it. Rule
> over the fish in the sea and the birds in the sky and
> over every living creature that moves on the ground."

While the main focus of this chapter is on the goodness of work in relationship to theological anthropology, the text above, and the larger context of the first two chapters of Genesis, tell us something important about God that we likely take for granted: God is a worker. While we may talk about wanting God to do work in our lives, we often miss the significance of the fact that God himself is a dutiful and thoughtful worker in the act of making the creation itself. The active language in

Genesis 1 ("Let there be...") indicates attention and purpose in God's creative activity. In Genesis 2, the language of "making" or "forming" the man from the dust of the ground as well as the literal surgical precision and craftwork in the making of Eve from Adam's rib tells us that work itself is creative, glorious, and dignified.

This work is verbally affirmed as "good" and "very good" by God in Genesis 1, and this is not only a matter of the goodness of work, but also beneficial for the creation itself. The truth about God as the ultimate worker is one of the most vital foundations for the goodness of work. The important dimensions of Genesis 1:26-28 include God's decision to make humans in his image and the implications of the function God has given humans as part of his creation.

There are many proposed views, some complementary with others, of what it means for humans to be created in the image of God. The emphasis on humans as those who function as rulers over the created order is among the most explicit, important, and most central questions of work. We cannot escape noticing that God intends humans to be those who are given what some of us call the first great commission: Humans are given the task and privilege of managing the world God created (some refer to humans as vice-regents). In this view humans are given work to do in God's world; work itself is woven into the expression of being one with the divine image.

But what does it mean to be rulers over the creation? While some

God himself is a *dutiful and thoughtful worker* in the act of making the creation itself.

have feared it means humans are given freedom to be careless and destructive of the created order, if we consider that it is God who gives humans responsibility for his creation, then we see this rulership over creation is an act of stewardship. When we link this specifically to our work, the language of stewardship means humans are accountable to God for the way we rule over the created order in our work itself. We can see this responsibility from a different angle in Genesis 2 where God places the man in the garden and gives him the responsibility for managing it. The creation accounts reveal that humans are divine image bearers who are created to work as stewards in God's world. To be given this responsibility and opportunity is truly an awesome privilege.

This stewardship is not merely an agricultural enterprise as it may appear at first glance. This first great commission includes all the ways that humans will work in and with the created order and extends to the various forms of work we have from construction to education to artistic work to law and beyond. These forms of work are opportunities to contribute to human flourishing; put another way, work that contributes to the good of God's world is one of the most primary expressions of being a divine image bearer.

DISTORTED BUT NOT OBLITERATED

The grand story includes a downward turn. In Genesis 3 humans succumb to the serpent's temptation and God pronounces a curse. Contrary to what may appear at first glance, the curse does not leave us with a view of work as something that is now a bad thing. There are two important aspects to emphasize here. First, we need to recognize how the curse induced distortions that can be truly horrific into the world. Second, we can also see the even with the entry of sin into the world, all is not lost, and work retains possibilities for goodness and flourishing.

When we consider the effects of the fall on work, we see how it illuminates the questions raised at the beginning of this chapter. One of the first things we can notice is the experience of work changes as a result of sin's entry into the world. In Genesis 3:17-19 God announces to Adam

> Because you listened to your wife and ate fruit from the tree about which I commanded you, 'You must not eat from it,'
>
> "Cursed is the ground because of you;
> through painful toil you will eat food from it
> all the days of your life.
>
> It will produce thorns and thistles for you,
> and you will eat the plants of the field.
>
> By the sweat of your brow
> you will eat your food
> until you return to the ground,
> since from it you were taken;
> for dust you are
> and to dust you will return.

The curse introduces toil, and now work will be accompanied by the experience of labor. Even in the best circumstances, work will not be unadulterated joy. The introduction of distress into work helps us understand the question above about those whose work is experienced as a kind of necessary evil or as "just a job." For many people in various kinds of jobs (manual labor, domestic work, levels of retail work, assembly line work, tedious desk work, etc.), this aspect of the fall is magnified in their daily experience. This challenge is not only an effect of what has happened to the experience of work itself, but also a dimension of what happens as an effect of fallenness on human perception. The fall complicates our experience and attitude toward work. The impact of sin can make us think work is contrary to the best

As the divine image remains with us, so does work itself as a component of our *essential dignity.*

THOUGH THE ENTRY OF <u>SIN IS REAL,</u> <u>ALL IS NOT LOST</u>. THE FALL <u>DOES NOT OBLITERATE</u> THE <u>IMAGE OF GOD</u> IN HUMANS.

<u>VINCENT BACOTE</u>

type of human life, even in times when work isn't a grind.

We can see further effects of sin in the world in the ways that work occurs in broken ways. This can help us as we think about why the long hangover of racism (personal and systemic) creeps into and complicates efforts to promote faith and work. The legacy of slavery and Jim Crow laws is one of the starkest ways we can see fallenness distort human relationships. Work connected to slavery can also be seen in the story of the Israelites. The book of Genesis ends with a great relationship between the Egyptians and Israelites, but at the beginning of Exodus (1:8-14) we see the emergence of a horrific turn of events. The Israelites were enslaved by the Egyptians and had "bitter lives" that became even more bitter when they were tasked with gathering the straw for making bricks and mortar (Exod 5:10-14). The Israelites were given work with horror woven into it, and many centuries later African-Americans experienced chattel slavery with its own brand of dehumanization linked to work. Work as God's idea is good, but post-fall distortions of work can be corrosive to human flourishing, with the added irony that the work performed by slaves may produce structures and products that are stunning to the eye and enjoyable in their use or consumption.

There are also oppressive and dissonant relationships between humans that lead to one of the problems of "otherness": those with power may see their people as fully human and full of potential while they come to believe that those enslaved or oppressed are deficiently human or subhuman and incapable of the best kinds of human achievements (of intellect, leadership, etc.).

The reality of the fall has reverberated through work life and been connected to sociopolitical dysfunctions like those connected with racism; when we consider how to convey the truth about humans as divine image bearers, the goodness of work and its connection to our life as Christians, we have to maintain an awareness of the way fallenness still complicates the message. For example, if we look at the language of worship and gratitude in Psalm 8, we see God praised for the tremendous privilege given to humans as those with the responsibility of ruling over God's world. As we saw above, this rulership is a form of stewardship that includes work that can lead to the flourishing of creation and is part of what it means to be a divine image bearer.

Though the entry of sin is real, all is not lost. The fall does not obliterate the image of God in humans. There are distortions in the expression of the image that occur, but the fact that all humans are image bearers means that a fundamental dignity remains with us. As the divine image remains with us, so does work itself as a component of our essential dignity, and as we see in the refrain that bookends Psalm 8: "Lord, our Lord, how majestic is your name in all the earth!" Our worship of God includes gratitude for the privilege of working as good stewards and even that work itself can be doxological. Unfortunately, sometimes Christians fall prey to the false belief that the curse in Genesis 3 means our work is now pure drudgery. They do not see that God never proclaimed work itself to be essentially bad. Yes, there is a curse, but the possibility of fruitful work remains.

A word about the doctrine of common grace is important here. "Common grace" is one way to talk about the fact that after the fall, it remains possible for us to still do the good work given to us in the first great commission. "Common" refers to the breadth and scale of God's work that allows us to continue our work, and "grace" refers to the fact that God was under no obligation to do this but chose to express this generosity to his creation. Common grace helps us see that good work can still be done that leads to human flourishing and gives us dignity.

REHUMANIZATION OF OUR WORK

The redemption that comes through Christ's work is truly good news. It is good news about the forgiveness of sin, reconciliation with God, and the promise of eternal life. It is even better news because it does not abandon the goodness of our work life given to us in the creation. Christ's incarnation provides an affirmation of the goodness of work. God the Son takes on flesh and identifies completely with us, including participation in work. It is easy to take for granted that Jesus inhabited the world of work for most of the years of his life (he was at least a carpenter, though one could argue that the term tekton, often translated "carpenter" could mean "craftsman" or "builder," terms with a greater scope). Just as the incarnation can be understood as clear evidence of God's commitment to his creation, it also implies that God reaffirms the fundamental goodness of work as part of the way humans function as divine image bearers.

Redemption also helps us see that all of our work, even without compensation, is for the good of our neighbor. When Jesus is asked about the greatest commandment in God's law, he answers by saying that it is really two commandments, love of God and love of neighbor. If we use the two great commandments as a lens for all of our life, including work, we can see that the purpose of work is not about the construction of our own fiefdoms or for selfish gain. While we benefit from our labor, work is a worshipful response to God that is for the good of our neighbors, whether the "neighbor" is as close as a spouse or as distant as customer on the other side of the globe.

Another important aspect of redemption is rooted in the Holy Spirit's work of regeneration and sanctification. While a doctrine like common grace can help us understand how good things can still happen in the world in spite of the fall (because of God's generosity to his creation in preservation of the earth and also the distribution of talents to humans), the Holy Spirit's work in regeneration and sanctification sets in motion a process we can regard as "rehumanization." We can get a sense of this in a text like Romans 8:5-6, which unveils the new possibility for life with God: "Those who live according to the flesh have their minds set on what the flesh desires; but those who live in accordance with the Spirit have their minds set on what the Spirit desires. The mind governed by the flesh is death, but the mind governed by the Spirit is life and peace."

To be governed by the Spirit does not imply an immediate experience of complete sanctification, but it does mean there is a new capacity for living in accordance with the ways of God. One way we can think about this as part of the re-humanization process is by expanding the way we typically think of what it means to be a spiritual person. Many Christians associate the idea of being spiritual with detachment from the world or with practices focused on our internal life. Another way to think of the spiritual person that resonates with this language in Romans 8 and connects with our original purpose as image bearers is to understand that "spiritual" means a human being made alive by the Holy Spirit, a human now able to be responsive to God and operate more in accordance with God's desires for us. We often think of this in terms of our internal character, which is extremely important, but this also extends to our ability to be those who can better operate as stewards of God's creation in the world of work.

Spiritual people in the workforce are certainly those characterized by traits such as integrity, honesty, and compassion. They can also be characterized as those whose faithfulness is expressed by actions such as creative contributions and innovative problem-solving in the workplace. This is one way we can understand the wonderful language in Ephesians 2:10 about good works given to us. When we benefit from redemption, we are those who are being transformed by God and oriented to do our work as a contribution to others (in contrast

Faithfulness is expressed
by actions such as
*creative contributions and
innovative problem-solving*
in the workplace.

to thinking of our work as somehow contributing to the foundation of our salvation).

The benefits of redemption open up possibilities for us to be more human in interactions with others in the workplace and to be those who seek to make the various environments of work more humanizing in their effects on fellow image bearers, especially when the specter of fallenness threatens to be the most dominant dimension of workplace ethos.

WORK THAT REFLECTS GOD'S KINGDOM

Our current experience of the redemption that comes in Christ is "already/not yet" where we know of and partly experience the promise of the ultimate reign of God that will come in the future while also experiencing the fall and its effects. When we live in this tension in our workplace contexts, we can experience confusion and wonder some days (or for some, most days) if our work really matters. The complete drama in Scripture can redirect us and modify our disposition when we take the end of the story seriously and see that life in the workplace is not an exercise in futility and vanity.

The implications of this for our perspective on the goodness of work are significant. A robust eschatology can encourage us to see our work as having the potential for greater fruitfulness than we imagine. Eschatology helps us envision work less characterized by the effects of a divided and broken world and orients us to see mundane work as a valuable contribution that is greater than it appears. God's promise to restore and renew his creation tells us that God is going to finish what he started, and when he started it included a great commission that included the privilege of work. When the fourth act of the drama arrives, God will completely humanize us, and that will include the way we work. In the meantime, we can consider how to at least gesture toward this future in our approach to work.

As we consider how to gesture toward this future, our participation in work plays a role in formation of character that will eventually be fully Christlike in the eschaton. What this means for now is that when we are doing work, we are participating in environments that we shape and that shape us. When we have an eschatological vision as part of our lens for work, we are more alert to the ways our lives and work environments are oriented toward the good of the kingdom or the negative resistance to God's reign. At the least we should be alert to the influence of systems on us and look for ways to cultivate our character, and (if possible) the work ethos itself. To have a vision for work that reflects God's kingdom is not the hubris of triumphalism but the thankful and hopeful efforts of humans who know God's complete story. This is a story that encourages us to keep doing work that serves him by serving fellow image bearers and making contributions that portend a future of which we now only have a glimpse.

The four-act drama contains reminders that God has truly given us a great thing in work. Aware of this, we can have a better frame for Christian formation and address the questions raised by my friends. The questions indicate serious problems in our world, but we are bearers of great news, and that is good news for the entirety of life. Are we willing to expand the faith and work conversation beyond its current audience and catalyze better formation of God's people as they worship and serve in our churches? May it be so and may greater humanization in our stewardship of work be a result.

———

Vincent Bacote is director of the Center for Applied Christian Ethics, associate professor of theology at Wheaton College, and is the author of The Political Disciple: A Theology of Public Life. *He lives in the Chicago area.*

Economic Wisdom:
Essential for Glorifying God and Loving Our Neighbor

GREG FORSTER

Growing in economic wisdom is essential for glorifying God and loving our neighbor. Jobs, poverty, globalization, environment, debt, racism, trade — does the church have anything to say about these matters, of such vital concern to the people around us? And how can we faithfully serve God in our daily work if we are ignorant of how the social systems of the economy are shaping our work? Economic wisdom is not only imperative for the mission of God to serve the well-being of the world around us, it is imperative for our own formation in Christlikeness. All day, every day, in our ordinary work, our work shapes the world. But our work also shapes us, and that means the world's systems will shape us as we work — unless we work with awareness of what is right and wrong within them.

I believe pastors today do not lack the will to speak about these matters. Our challenge is to find language pastors can use with confidence, a way of bearing witness for neighbor-love, for justice and mercy, that does not make the church captive to partisan or ideological agendas. Finding new language to reconnect our moral commitments to public problems in times of polarization and ideological dead-ends is something the church has always been doing. And we can do it now.

THE BIBLE OVERCOMES OUR POLARIZATION

Most pastors today seem reluctant to get specific in this area. They're comfortable telling us to be just and fair. But few are able to articulate what a just society with a just economy would look like, or which specific aspects of our social order today are unjust.

It's not difficult to guess why. Our society is so politicized, and its politics are so polarized, that it is difficult to get specific about public issues without appearing to take sides in bitter partisan and ideological conflicts. If pastors begin denouncing specific unjust practices or recommending specific kinds of social order, people may think they're importing worldly political and economic ideologies into the church.

Pastors are right to be concerned about captivity to worldly ideologies and partisan conflicts. But silence and paralysis are not adequate responses either. God's love and holiness cry out for a witness in the face of the world's complacency and wickedness. And how foolish do we look, telling people that they need to repent from sin or that Jesus will make them righteous, while we remain passive in the face of the challenges and injustices that these same people face daily?

To meet the challenge of our times, we must find some way to talk about justice without becoming captive to partisan or ideological agendas. Here, as everywhere else, the Bible gives us the power to walk in freedom as children of God. Because the Bible is God's Word, it has the authority to provide us with purpose, meaning, standards, and priorities that cut through the world's narrow agendas.

As we draw this freedom from the Bible, we must bear two issues in mind: The Bible was written at a time when economic systems were different, and the Bible is not a technical manual that will tell us, for example, what the tax rate should be. We face these kinds of concerns whenever we apply the Bible to contemporary life. But, in our time, they are especially urgent and sensitive in the area of economic wisdom, given the politicization and polarization of our culture.

It would be wise for pastors to avoid too much detail in the pulpit. It is not necessary to take a stand on the particulars of most public policies. Pastors shouldn't try to substitute for the professional expertise of economists, lawyers, politicians, and policymakers. And they should be mindful that the more we get into granular detail, the more cautious we have to be about how fallible human judgment shapes our thinking.

However, pastors can and must help people interpret the meaning of their lives and their world. The biblical witness gives pastors tools to do this in the following ways (among others):

- **Purpose:** The story, laws and promises of the Bible reveal which economic purposes are good and which are not.
- **Meaning:** The church helps people develop a hermeneutic of life based on the Bible's witness, which changes how they understand their daily participation in economic systems.
- **Standards:** The Bible shows us the protective ethical boundaries that God provided for our economic behavior.
- **Priorities:** The story, law, and promises of the Bible help us put first things first.

Cumulatively, this becomes a good opportunity for preachable witness to economic wisdom!

Above, I referred to the "story, law, and promises" of the Bible. We need each of these for a full application of the Bible's witness to economic justice.

The story of the Bible provides the interpretive framework we need to understand its law and promises. Our daily lives must be reinterpreted in light of God's action in creating us to be good stewards of his world, working together with one another in holy love. God's redemptive action, restoring us to joy, peace, and righteousness in Christ by the blood of the cross, points the way back to that kind of life in our economic activities — and the way forward as well, as we live in anticipation of the glorification of all things in Jesus' return.

The **law** of the Bible, its commands, provides the explicit substance of its witness to neighbor-love, justice, and mercy. Scott Rae, in a book chapter that does an admirable job of summarizing the content of the Bible's economic commands, offers three clear ways these teachings apply to us today:

- "The economic system should maximize the opportunities for human beings to exercise creativity, initiative and innovation – what we might call 'human capital.'"
- "The economic system is to provide a means for human beings to support themselves and their dependents – that is, to provide access to the world's productive resources."
- "The economic system...must take care of those who cannot take care of themselves."[31]

The **promises** of the Bible are the basis on which we go forward into the world to carry out God's purposes. We rely on his promise of restorative grace to us individually, giving us strength and spiritual insight to navigate our contemporary challenges. We rely on his promise of restorative grace to us corporately, as the church, working cooperatively to build a Christian witness to justice. And we rely on his promise that he is already at work, invisibly, in all of the world around us. As we go out into the world to follow God, we are not taking him there but joining him there, in a creative and redemptive mission that he is already advancing.

WITNESS TO ECONOMIC WISDOM – PAST AND FUTURE
Heroes of the faith throughout church history have made justice for the poor and the oppressed central to their gospel witness. The early fathers of the church spoke out frequently against the ruling class who

gained and protected their wealth and power through brutal subjugation of ordinary workers — so fiercely that, as we read them today, they often seem to be talking as if good use of wealth and power is not even a possibility.[32] The theological scholars of the Middle Ages treated economic ethics as a topic of critical importance; the late Middle Ages in particular saw an explosion of theological interest in economic ethics.[33] Martin Luther's famous 95 Theses on the sale of indulgences deployed the spiritual power of the gospel to liberate the poor and oppressed from a system of economic exploitation.[34] The Reformation doctrine of vocation led Luther and other reformers, such as John Calvin, to make economic justice a key pastoral and theological concern.[35] John Wesley preached extensively on justice for the poor and the oppressed, challenging the traditional abuses of the landed aristocratic hierarchy and also supporting reform of the treatment of workers in newly emerging industrial factories.[36] Across the Atlantic, his Great Awakening contemporary Jonathan Edwards also made economic ethics a high priority in preaching and practice.[37] More recently, Martin Luther King, Jr.'s witness against ethnic injustice was extensively bound up with witness against economic injustice.[38]

The modern economy we live in is in large part a product of this Christian witness. Throughout the world, as far back as history records, economies were structured on master/slave and ruler/subject hierarchies. Only a few people — perhaps two percent of the population — had public protection for their rights to own property and do business without other people's arbitrary control. And for all those thousands of years, precisely because the economy was suppressed by injustice, every society in history was materially poor. Almost all people lived either at bare subsistence level or close enough that a bad year would put them there. This was the universal state of human economy until the last two centuries, as rights to participate in the economy were gradually (and, of course, incompletely) extended beyond the tiny ruling class to more and more citizens. One of the major forces behind that change, and the resulting explosion of material wealth, was the influence of Christianity. Its public witness to the equal human dignity of all people, and to the calling God has for all people in their daily work, demanded the extension of economic rights to more people. And the extension of rights led to the explosion of wealth, as the productive capacities of image-bearing human beings was finally permitted to get to work serving the common good.[39]

However, this new economic order, with its freedom and growth, has created new moral challenges. And the legacy of past injustices continues to be with us in agonizing ways. Although slavery and ethnic prejudice are universal practices in fallen human culture, Europe's colonization of other parts of the world in the early modern period, resulting in industrial-scale enslavement and the hideous delusion of racial manifest destiny, is a unique phenomenon.[40] Formal, legal systems of injustice have been removed, but racism remains with us, and we have also inherited unequal distributions of what economists call "human capital" (e.g. skills, knowledge, experience) and "social capital" (e.g. networks of relationships).

Another challenge is sexuality. Increased wealth and widespread access to markets have made sexual immorality much cheaper, both financially and socially; the breakdown of marriage is one of the primary factors contributing to economic poverty today.[41] On a deeper level, the decline of sexual morality is part of, and reinforces, a more general decline of public moral norms that has a widespread disordering impact on the economy.[42] No one pretends to have easy answers to these and other painful problems, but it is the church's job to be figuring out how to cope with them and alleviate injustice and brokenness as best we can by God's grace.

Also, as our society became more secular over the course of the 20th century, materialistic and worldly understandings of economic systems have grown more prevalent. Secular conservatives tend to view "the market" as an automatically self-correcting system that operates by the equivalent of natural laws, requiring no basis in transcendent moral and metaphysical commitments or ties of community. Secular progressives tend to view all people's behavior, relationships, opportunities, and challenges as merely a function of their access to material resources, which can be expanded by the technocratic state — often in ways that harm rather than strengthen human relationships and community.

Libertarians tend to view the economy as a result of radically free and autonomous human choice, unconstrained by any limitations of history, culture, family or (above all) moral defects in the human heart. Communitarians tend to view all economic exchange outside local communities as morally deforming, undervaluing the norms of universal goodwill and cooperation that were essential in the emergence of global markets. All Christians should become aware of which kinds of economic idolatry they personally tend toward and adopt practices to help them continue discovering blind spots and learning from those with different perspectives.

THEMES OF ECONOMIC WISDOM

How then can we talk about economic wisdom without captivity to worldly systems? We need a body of language that grows out of trans-partisan moral commitments — that is, language that is morally serious but that does not commit the speaker to one side or the other in any partisan or ideological divide. Such a body of language can only grow out of communities of Christians who come together across those boundaries, not for the purpose of debating but for the purpose of building moral consensus. Debates are necessary and useful in their proper place. But if the only thing we do is debate, it tends to exaggerate differences and create the impression that there is no common ground. To debate our differences is one necessary part of the process of building moral consensus, but it must not become the whole of that process or even the dominant component. The primary question is: "Where can we shake hands and agree on what must be done, so we can roll up our sleeves and get to work?"

For almost 10 years, the Oikonomia Network (ON) has been steward-

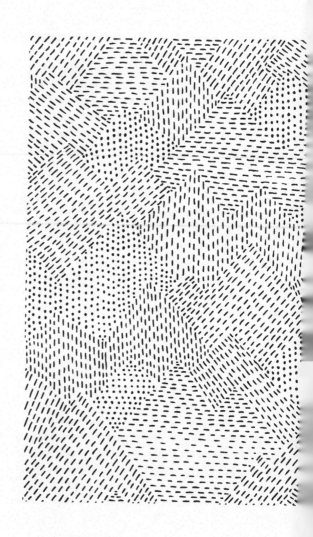

The purpose of work is to serve human needs in response to God's creative and redemptive activity.

GREG FORSTER

As God redeems us, _he empowers us to reorient the world toward him_ through our work.

ing this kind of conversation. The ON is a community of theological educators dedicated to whole-life discipleship and God's calling for all people to fruitful work. The ON has been known from the beginning that our daily work takes place in economic systems, and that existing conversations in our area of service about how Christians can evaluate and speak into economic systems were unhelpfully partisan or ideological. So, the ON has slowly built a new conversation.

The result is the Economic Wisdom Project (economicwisdom.org), a collection of resources that express ON's commitment to Christian witness in economic life. The vision paper that lays out ON's principles, "A Christian Vision for Flourishing Communities," is organized around four major themes and 12 elements of economic wisdom:

Stewardship and Flourishing: God created human beings to be good stewards of this world. We carry out that stewardship when we do work that helps God's world flourish. The fall has infected our work with toil and frustration, but our "to-do list" remains the same: Do work that serves others and cultivate blessings out of the raw materials God provides. As God redeems us, he empowers us to reorient the world toward him through our work. The economic institutions that define the cultural meaning of our work provide the essential background for that journey.

1. We have a stewardship responsibility to flourish in our own lives, to help our neighbors flourish as fellow stewards, and to pass on a flourishing economy to future generations.
2. Economies flourish when people have integrity and trust each other.
3. In general, people flourish when they take responsibility for their own economic success by doing work that serves others and makes the world better.

Value Creation: Just as God is a unity of diverse persons, we (made in his image) were created to live and act in relationship and community. So, if we are made for work, we are made for the economy — the vast web of human relationships in which people exchange their work with one another. The purpose of work is to serve human needs in response to God's creative and redemptive activity; in economic terms, work that serves human needs creates value. Work draws us into voluntary cooperation with others, creating value for one another in networks of interdependence. Through market exchange, we become coworkers with millions of people!

4. Real economic success is about how much value you create, not how much money you make.
5. A productive economy comes from the value-creating work of free and virtuous people.
6. Economies generally flourish when policies and practices reward value creation.

Productivity and Opportunity: The economy is a moral system. What kind of economy we have will depend on what kind of people we are; and what kind of people we are is also impacted by what kind of economy we have. The foundation of a flourishing economy is the productive work of free and virtuous people. The fall affects this social system at both the individual and structural levels, but the underlying pattern remains. An economy that prioritizes productive service and opportunity will help cultivate love, joy, and contentment; an economy that prioritizes short-term gratification will tend to produce shallow, selfish people.

7. Households, businesses, communities, and nations should support themselves by producing more than they consume.

8. A productive economy lifts people out of poverty and generally helps people flourish.

9. The most effective way to turn around poverty, economic distress, and injustice is by expanding opportunity for people to develop and deploy their God-given productive potential in communities of exchange, especially through entrepreneurship.

Responsible Action: Christians follow Christ in exercising the offices of prophet, priest and king. Prophetically, the church is uniquely shaped by the Word and Spirit, which includes its witness against injustice and a special care for the poor. In its priestly role, the church restores the Christward orientation humans were created for, including in our economic activity. Kingship calls upon us to promote responsible stewardship within and over the creation order; this means being hopeful, but not indulging in wishful thinking. Our challenge is to be bold for the kingdom and resist complacency, while also respecting the God-given integrity of natural and social systems and being realistic about the fall and our own limitations.

10. Programs aimed at economic problems need a fully rounded understanding of how people flourish.

11. Economic thinking must account for long-term effects

and unintended consequences.
12. In general, economies flourish when goodwill is universal and global, but control is local, and personal knowledge guides decisions.

We also identify five pathways of pastoral application. These specify how "the rubber hits the road" for economic wisdom in a local church. One is theology; economic wisdom is closely bound up with Christian doctrine, from the Trinity and the incarnation to redemption and the kingdom, and we are not effectively teaching the message of Christianity if we do not connect it to the way people live their lives all day. Another is pastoral care; economic wisdom is essential to helping people make sense of their lives and know how to live them. A third is compassion; too much of our effort to "help" the materially impoverished actually harms them, because we lack the economic wisdom to join the poor as equal partners in flourishing. A fourth is the common good; growing efforts to connect the church to the good of the communities in which we find ourselves has brought us face to face with the desperate need for wisdom about economic matters. A final pathway is youth and family. In a culture that offers young people many invitations to private self-indulgence and public idolatries, but few authentic callings to which they could really give their lives in practice, economic wisdom is essential to offering the rising generation a vision of Christian life that can stick.

PASTORS MUST PREACH ABOUT ECONOMIC WISDOM
Speaking out for the cause of neighbor-love in our economic life is central to being a good pastor. This responsibility is part of the Christian life for all of us, of course. All Christians are called to be prophets, priests, and kings. But this is particularly important for those who are professional spokespeople for the kingdom of God. The gospel call to repentance from sin becomes trite and superficial if the institutional church is not putting forward a powerful vision of justice and mercy

that stands in sharp contrast to the darkness and evil of the world.

One thing is certain: You may not be interested in the economy, but the economy is interested in you. The spiritual formation of the faithful takes place mostly through their daily work in the economy, and the outside world is watching to see if the church has anything to say about these vital matters of life-and-death importance to the common good. The good news is that God is interested in the economy and has given us the Word and Spirit we need to develop wisdom about how to live in it and how to speak into it. And he has given us one another, so we can learn together. Discipling believers into a Christ-centered economic life is at the heart of the church's challenge today; praise God that he has equipped us so abundantly for it!

———

Greg Forster is the director of the Oikonomia Network and author of seven books, including Joy for the World *and* The Church on Notice. *Forster lives in Pleasant Prairie, Wisconsin.*

The Local Church:
Uniquely Designed and Empowered to Promote Human Flourishing

TOM NELSON

Almost every time I pull up to the intersection, I see him. His dirty tattered clothes and tired disheveled appearance communicates to those willing to give him even momentary eye contact, a lack of human flourishing. As the light turns red, he holds up a carefully crafted cardboard hand-written sign, "homeless, need help." I do not know his name and seeing him standing there I wonder about his life story. Rain, snow, or shine this fellow image bearer is a regular fixture on my morning commutes.

As we live our daily lives it is not uncommon for us to encounter the homeless. We may simply walk by them on a busy street, encounter them in a park during our evening stroll, or as we stop at a local intersection. While we may differ on what a proper individual and societal response should be to the growing homeless population,[43] we would

agree homelessness does not lead to human flourishing. Food, cloth-
ing, and shelter are vital to human wellbeing, yet home is not merely a
place of provision; it is also a place of belonging. Embedded within us
is a deep longing to know and be known. As image bearers of God, we
were created not just to exist as isolated individuals, but also to belong
to a community. To truly flourish, we need a place to call home and a
people we call family.

When it comes to flourishing, what is true in the physical realm is
also true in the spiritual realm. Christian spirituality devoid of local
church community is a homeless faith. A homeless faith is an impoverished faith, for we were created and redeemed with community in
mind. Craig Van Gelder insightfully writes,

> Defining salvation in individual terms is biblical, but
> it is not all that the bible teaches. The Spirit of God is
> creating a new community as the body of Christ. While
> salvation is always individual in its effect, how it is to
> be offered and experienced is very corporate. To be
> converted to Christ is to be converted to his body the
> church.[44]

Yet in a culture embracing individualistic spirituality, we often devalue
local church commitment as if it is a convenient option and not an
essential of a vibrant faith.

This is not to say skeptical sentiment regarding the local church is
not without merit. At times churches fall short of God's design and
spiritual vitality. All too often churches advocate a compartmentalized
way of being rather than an integral, seamless, and coherent faith. Who
has not been part of a local faith community that reinforced a faulty
sacred/secular dichotomy, suffered mission drift, and failed to meet
its own high ideals? Yet is living a homeless faith a better path forward
in our quest for human flourishing?

I often hear advocates of a homeless faith say things like, "I love

Jesus, but I don't do church," or "I worship Jesus when I am out in nature," or "I am not into organized religion," or "My Bible study group is my church," or "I listen to sermons online." While these activities and experiences may be good endeavors, they are not the same as an embodied faith lived out in a local church home among a local people we call our church family. The gospel properly understood not only makes it possible for us to be reconciled with God and others, it welcomes us into a new family, the local church.[45]

DOES THE LOCAL CHURCH REALLY MATTER?

The question of whether or not the local church really matters is often raised both explicitly and implicitly. I believe the local church matters more than we may realize. First, the local church is God's plan A. Second, the local church promotes human flourishing. Third, the local church is the love of Jesus' heart.

The Local Church is God's Plan A

Why the church? While we could answer this question in a myriad of ways, most compelling is the church is Jesus' idea. Jesus declares, "I will build my church and the gates of hell will not prevail against it."[46] Jesus declares his redemptive plan for restoring a broken world is the church. But what is the church?

In Matthew's Gospel, the word translated church means "called out ones."[47] The New Testament portrays the reality of the church in two overlapping dimensions, both local and universal. The universal church is composed of all believers no matter where they are located both in space and time. The local church refers to a particular assembly of believers located in a particular place. Often the universal church is referred to as the invisible church and the local church as the visible church.[48] The New Testament emphasizes the local dimension as the primary dimension, but there are periodic glimpses and reminders of the local church's transcendent connection to a larger, but not more important reality.[49] When we contemplate the proportionality of New

The local church has always been and continues to be *God's plan A for redeeming a broken world*.

Testament teaching on the church we see the local church is front and center.

The Primacy of the Local Church

Making a case for the primacy of the local church, Miroslav Volf emphasizes the importance of proximity and place. Volf writes,

> For the people of God, gathering at one place constitutes the primary subject of ecclesiality...the church is not simply an act of assembling, rather it assembles at a specific place. It is the people who in a specific way assemble at a specific place.[50]

One way the primacy of the local church is seen in the New Testament is how the early followers of Jesus understood Jesus' proclamation to build his church (Matt 16:18) and his Great Commission (Matt 28:18-20) to make disciples of all peoples to the ends of the earth. As the book of Acts unfolds, the apostolic strategy to take the gospel to the ends of the earth is centered in establishing local churches throughout the Roman Empire. While the book of Acts reports a great number of individuals embracing the gospel, the primary missional thrust was birthing and sustaining of local churches.

The apostles viewed the establishment, development, and multiplication of vibrant local churches at the heart of the gospel-centered, disciple-making mission Christ commissioned them to embrace and the Holy Spirit empowered them to accomplish. The local church has always been and continues to be God's plan A for redeeming a broken world. As God's plan A, the local church is uniquely empowered, brilliantly designed, and strategically positioned.

Supernaturally Empowered

The pouring out of the Holy Spirit at Pentecost was a direct fulfillment of Jesus' promise for supernatural empowerment of his global, gospel mission.[51] The varieties of spiritual gifts given to the church as a gospel-shaped, Spirit-filled community is also evidence of the supernatural empowerment of the local church.[52] In local church community we encounter the manifest presence of Christ in a unique way. Martyred German pastor, Dietrich Bonhoeffer writes that "Christianity means community through Jesus Christ and in Jesus Christ. No Christian community is more or less than this."[53] Is it any wonder the New Testament writer of Hebrews warns followers of Jesus not to neglect gathering together in local church community (Heb 10:25).

Brilliantly Designed

The local church is not only supernaturally empowered; the church is also brilliantly designed. As the master architect, Jesus created both an organic and institutional entity, one that would be a faithful presence in a community and have multigenerational continuity over time. Integral to Jesus' design was a new community flourishing in a living ecosystem embodying a thick moral ecology teeming with diversity and vitality. Unlike anything else in the world, from cradle to grave, the local church is designed to promote human flourishing across all cultural contexts, generations, and ethnicities. When we look back at two thousand years of church history, we are in awe of how the local church has not only survived in the most varied and hostile of cultures, but also continues to thrive today against opposition and persecution. The stunning resilience of the local church over such a wide span of time and cultures speaks convincingly of the church's supernatural provenance, providential care, and brilliant design.

Strategically Positioned

Jesus not only designed the local church; he also strategically positioned it for ongoing impact. Imagine if we developed a great product that would really help people flourish. How would we get that product out to the greatest number of people? We probably would not invent our own distribution system. Instead we would look for a vast distribution system already in place. We may look for online opportunities, but we would also look for stores like Wal-Mart and Target that are present in virtually every community in America. With more than 5,000 Wal-Marts and more than 1,800 Targets in the United States we would do everything we could to get our products on their store shelves.

Yet when it comes to our mission of making disciples, we are quick to sidestep or ignore the strategic positioning of the local church. In the United States alone, there are more than 300,000 local Protestant churches and 25,000 Catholic parishes. This massive distribution system makes Wal-Mart and Target puny in comparison. In almost every nook and cranny of our country, in urban, suburban, and rural communities there are local churches. Some are withering and dying, some are stagnating or just maintaining. Yet the often-untold story is the great number of local churches that are being birthed, renewed, and thriving.

It is tempting when we are frustrated with the local church to rein-

The local church is not only supernaturally empowered; the church is also _brilliantly designed_.

vent a new parachurch distribution system, but wisdom tells us we ought to utilize better what is already there. The local church needs continual renewal, but it must not be sidestepped or abandoned. Like families that can be difficult, dysfunctional, and in need of nurture and care, so too are local churches. Family life is filled with broken, sinful people and lived out in the suffering of a badly broken world. We don't give up on family life because it is difficult or disappointing.

Instead we work to renew and restore families because God designed the family to be and do what no other institution can do. The same is true for the local church. With more than two billion adherents to Christianity globally, the local church's supernatural empowerment, unique design, and strategic positioning is evident. The local church is God's plan A; we simply do not see a plan B in the inspired pages of Scripture.

The Local Church and Human Flourishing
God's plan for human flourishing is not a mystery. The two divine institutions of the family and the church transcend time and culture. In creation, we see God's good design of the family, and in redemption we see God's good design of the local church. The path to human flourishing makes its meandering way to the local church.

God's plan for human flourishing is not a mystery.

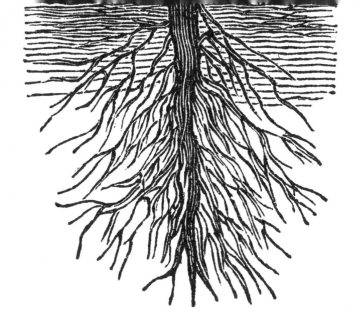

The family
and the church
transcend time
and culture.

TOM NELSON

Yet when we see ourselves as spiritual consumers, we view the local church like a gas station, a place we cruise into one day a week in order to fill up our spiritual tanks. We may also see the local church like a movie theatre, a time for us to be entertained and distracted from the difficulties of our lives. For some the local church is like a drug store, dispensing just the right prescription or therapy that will numb our pain. For many, the local church is more like a box retailer that has everything we want under one roof, neatly organized, easily accessible, and placed conveniently on a lower shelf.[54]

While there is nothing wrong with a local church meeting human felt needs, these distorted views of the church focus on individual wants and needs rather than the biblical idea of the church, transforming us, centering on the needs of others, and advancing the mission of God in the world.

How are we to view the local church and its role in human flourishing? A primary way the New Testament helps us see the local church is through metaphors and analogies. Edmund Clowney explains in his research how there are more than 96 figures and analogies applied to the church in the New Testament.[55] Two New Testament metaphors deserve special reflection, describing the local church as the household of God and the body of Christ.

The Household of God

The Apostle Paul reminds Timothy that as God's household, the local church as a new covenant community is God's family.[56] Paul speaks of the local church at Corinth as "God's building.[57]" The apostle Peter utilizes language of the church as "living stones, a spiritual house, and a holy priesthood."[58] Peter also describes the church as "a chosen race, a royal priesthood, and a holy nation."[59]

I often hear people say, "The church is people, not a building." While the church is about people, it is also about place. Human souls matter, but so do buildings, brick, and mortar. The building and household metaphors remind us the local church is an institution with a sense of place, enduring stability, aesthetic beauty, and functional purpose. The church is a gathering place for gospel transformed people to belong, a place to call home. When we understand the church as a family, we embrace a coherent faith, a beautiful tapestry of people and place woven together by the Spirit into a new community. The local church is not merely a place we go, it is designed to be a place we call home and a people we call family.

The Body of Christ

Another metaphor illuminating the local church is the body of Christ. The Apostle Paul writes, "And he (Jesus) put all things in subjection under his feet and gave him as head over all things to the church, which is his body, the fullness of him who fills all in all," (Eph 1:23). Paul's comparison of the church to the human body and its living, breathing, interdependent, symbiotic systems are rich with meaning and significance. As the body of Christ, the local church is a conduit of Christ's resurrection power and presence.

The Church and Whole Life Discipleship

Discipleship and spiritual formation are anything but a solitary enterprise, but deeply communal and widely comprehensive in nature. Spiritual formation in Christ-likeness is designed to take place not only on an individual level, but within immersion in spiritual community. Discipleship in Christ informs and permeates every nook and cranny of human existence. The local church was designed by Christ and empowered by the Holy Spirit with this in mind. As gospel transformed people, we grow in Christ not like a single solitary tree, but more as an interconnected grove of trees, planted together in the proximity of local church community.

In our journey of discipleship, we must move from thinking just "me" to embracing "we." Psychiatrist Curt Thompson offers helpful wisdom as he takes into consideration both the teaching of Scripture and the latest neuroscience research. Thompson emphasizes the

I was more concerned
about my parishioners
joining my place of work
on Sunday than I was
about *equipping them*
for their place of work
on Monday.

essential place of spiritual community in healing and flourishing as
we move from disintegrated lives to more integrated persons. Thompson writes, "Paul speaks of believers as Jesus' body. As we engage this
role, we come to a place of deep integration of the "we" and "I." This
is what it means to be the body of Christ."[60]

It is in the context of local church community that our journey
to increasing integral wholeness finds resonance in the life-giving
relationships and vocational stewardships of everyday life. Within
local church community we have the capacity and empowerment to
incarnate The Cultural Mandate,[61] The Great Commandment (Matt
22:37-40) and The Great Commission (Matt 28:18-20). In local church
community we embrace the transforming invitation to be yoked with
Jesus and learn from him as his apprentices (Matt 11:28-30).

In community we learn the precepts and practices of Jesus. As we
learn from Jesus, through the power of the Holy Spirit, we pursue
spiritual disciplines of engagement and withdrawal of both solitude

and service.[62] Whole life discipleship leads us to virtuous lives and communities that are salt and light in the world. The Apostle Peter reminds us that gospel transformation involves virtue. Peter writes, "For this reason make every effort to supplement your faith with virtue...[63]" It is the distinct virtuous lives of Christ followers that play a vital role in advancing the common good and making the truths of the gospel plausible to an increasingly secular age.[64] Jesus reminded his followers collectively they are salt and light in the world. As salt and light, distinct in virtue as well as good work, their lives lived in new creation community will prompt others to glorify God.[65]

The virtue acquisition and transformation that takes place within local church life has far reaching influence on all dimensions of life, both at work and at home. For example, extensive research has shown that couples regularly attending worship services at a local faith community have greater marital stability, happiness, and harmony.[66] As a disciple-making enterprise, the local church is the primary catalyst for healing, formation, and human flourishing. Nothing can surpass the local church, and nothing can replace it.

A Church for Monday

For many years as a pastor I committed pastoral malpractice. That may seem shocking, but it is true. Due to an impoverished theology, I embraced a faulty pastoral vocational paradigm. There was a large Sunday to Monday gap in my thinking. The tragic result was my congregation was spiritually malformed and our discipleship mission was impoverished. I knew pastors were to equip the church for the work of service. The problem was my flawed understanding of what this work of service entailed. My focus had been on equipping my parishioners to serve well within the church rather than equipping them for serving well in the world where God had called them throughout the week.

I was more concerned about my parishioners joining my place of work on Sunday than I was about equipping them for their place of work on Monday. So, I did what pastors are reluctant to do. I confessed to my congregation my failure. I confessed I had spent the majority of my time equipping them for the minority of their lives. That was now going to change. Now I would be concentrating on equipping my congregation for the various callings they had during the week. It was not that the gathered church on Sunday didn't matter anymore, it clearly did, but what now also mattered was the scattered church on Monday.

When clergy have an impoverished vocational paradigm, congregants are inevitably malformed, and the disciple-making mission of the church is hindered. Is the local church's primary focus Sunday or Monday? I believe the primary focus must be Monday. What does a church for Monday look like? A church for Monday embraces a robust work and vocational theology recognizing that a primary work of the church is the church at work.[67] A church for Monday cultivates a liturgical regularity celebrating the priesthood of all believers and highlighting parishioners' daily lives.[68] Pastoral praxis changes in a local church that has Monday in mind. Pastoral practice not only includes hospital visits to care for parishioners who are ill, but also workplace visits to understand and encourage parishioners in their daily work. A pastor who equips with Monday in mind addresses their own vocational insularity by placing a greater priority to learn about the various vocational callings of their parishioners.

Faith, Work, and Economic Wisdom

When a church is focused on Monday, church leaders increasingly grasp the importance of how biblical teaching calls a local faith community to live out a growing neighborly love of both Christ like compassion and economic capacity.[69] The stewardship of the local church as an economic actor within a community[70] is taken seriously, addressing matters of economic development and injustice. An entrepreneurial spirit among the membership is encouraged and celebrated. An economics of mutuality embedded in a free market system informs a triple bottom line not merely of profit maximization, but of human flourishing and planet sustainability.[71] A local church is called to care not only for its members but seek the flourishing of all members of its community, placing a high value on the most vulnerable.[72] The local church matters more than we might think. It is designed to promote human flourishing, and it is the love of Jesus' heart.

The Love of Jesus' Heart

As a pastor, I love officiating weddings. One of my favorite moments of a wedding is when I stand next to the groom in front of the church waiting for his bride to come down the aisle. While all eyes are on the bride, I often glance at the groom. His heart is beating fast, his eyes are often glistening with tears and there is nothing or no one he loves and cherishes more than his bride coming down the aisle.

The description of the church as the bride of Christ captures this kind of heart affection and passion. The Apostle Paul paints a tender picture of the church as the cherished bride of Christ.[73] The Apostle John in his glorious revelation of Jesus and the consummation at the end of time speaks of the joyful marriage of the supper of the Lamb and his bride, the church.[74]

It is no mystery what Jesus loves most. The bride metaphor helps us to grasp at the heart level how Jesus loves his church, warts and all. The most reliable indicator of authentic faith is not merely what a person believes, but what a person truly loves. The closer we walk with Jesus, the more we capture his heart and the more we love what he loves. Jesus passionately loves and cherishes the local church. How about us? When we love Jesus' bride, the local church, we will speak well of her, enthusiastically serve her, sacrificially support her, and make time in our busy schedules for our brothers and sisters in Christ in our local faith community.

Our greatest problem with the local church may not be a head problem, but a heart problem. Perhaps we need to confess our improperly ordered loves. Have we, in attitude and action, loved Jesus' bride as we ought? Maybe we not only need to make a renewed commitment to Jesus, but also a renewed commitment to his local church. Maybe it is time to say no to a homeless faith and come home to local church community.

COMING HOME

Jesus' parable of the prodigal sons reminds us there is no place like home. While the younger son left his home to go to a far country, the older son stayed at home but was not fully at home. We may be a prodigal in not having yet come home to Christ as our personal Lord and Savior, but we also may be a prodigal who having embraced Christ has not yet fully come home to the local church. When it comes to local church community we may be in far country, or we may be in church every Sunday, just going through the motions, but not fully there. We may be living a homeless faith and not even realize our impoverished condition. Perhaps it is time to come home to a gospel-centered, disciple-making local church where Christ is honored, and his comprehensive kingdom mission is embraced and embodied with heart, mind, and hands. There is no place like home.

———

Tom Nelson is president of Made to Flourish and senior pastor of Christ Community Church. He serves on the leadership team of the Oikonomia Network, and lives in the Kansas City area.

Conclusion: Now What?

LUKE BOBO

We began with the Bible's Big Story. Why? Perhaps Alasdair MacIntyre can help. He argues that before we can answer the question, "What am I to do?" we must first answer, "Of what story or stories do I find myself a part?"[75] In other words, the stories or story we find ourselves in forms us. Stories inform our beliefs and behaviors; stories inform our worldview and our workview.[76] Stories are not benign. Incomplete stories, incoherent stories can deform us — our thinking and our concomitant actions. Incoherent stories that perpetuate a secular versus spiritual divide is damaging, for example. The church has perpetuated a dwarf-size version of the Big Story that has traditionally only included the fall and redemption. Such a version of the Big Story is primarily focused on personal evangelism and securing a ticket to heaven. Such a version of the Big Story can stunt the growth of believers and skew how we see. However, a fuller, integrated, and complete story that includes four movements of the grand narrative — creation, the fall, redemption and consummation — reorients us to the truths of the Bible and moves us, progressively, toward an integrated life. A coherent Big Story reorients us to God's mission, to the importance of pursuing personal wholeness, to God's view on work, to the necessity of growing in economic wisdom, and to the role of the local church.

The mission of God is cosmic in scope. It includes both the redemption of individuals and the redemption of institutions that impede the flourishing of human beings. Appropriating the Big Story means working to balance the scales of justice for all persons because Lady Justice is sometimes partial. Appropriating the Big Story means fighting to overcome systemic-isms like racism, ageism, sexism, and xenophobism, which are woven into the fabric of our society and its institutions.

The Bible's Big Story, of which we find ourselves, means embracing the harsh reality that all human beings have suffered massive disintegration. Our loves and affections are distorted. That is why the Apostle Paul speaks for all Christians in Romans 7 when he states, "the good that we should do, we abandon in favor of doing evil." The Big Story reminds us that we participate with God in becoming whole or integrated persons. The Big Story invites us to yoke ourselves with Jesus as an apprentice, and the Big Story invites us to gather friends of virtue, among other things, to aid us to becoming whole persons.

The grand narrative teaches us that all work, except sinful work, is good, contributive, and noble. This work matters greatly in God's economy. The stay-at-home dad's work matters and benefits his children; a janitor's work matters and benefits those who use various facilities; the Uber driver's work matters and benefits her passengers; and the pastor's work matters and benefits his parishioners. There is no pecking order of occupations or vocations in God's workview.

Growing in economic wisdom is another tenet we glean from the pages of the Bible. Wise economic actors aid and abet the flourishing of their neighbors, their neighborhoods, and their cities. God is deeply concerned about the economy because it is chiefly a human enterprise. Pastors nor parishioners can neglect this moral system. Rather, pastors and parishioners must grow in their economic discernment and seize opportunities to join God in making what is unjust, just and what is unrighteous, righteous for the flourishing of the most vulnerable in our society.

The Big Story of Scripture, of which we find ourselves, means embracing, perhaps anew, the unique and divine role of the local church. God has prepared and equipped the church, his bride, to actively participate in the renewal of all things. And while God's renewal project is cosmic in scope, the scattered church can, nonetheless, participate in this grand renewal project by doing our daily and weekly work well.

We humbly and graciously urge you, in the power of the Holy Spirit, to appropriate these six foundations — living by the grand narrative of Scripture, participating in the mission of God, pursuing personal wholeness, engaging in work that leads to human flourishing, growing in economic wisdom, and supporting God's Plan A — the local church — to undergird your journey toward an integrated life.

———

Luke Bobo serves as director of curriculum and resources for Made to Flourish and brings leadership to creating and curating resources and curriculum for our network of pastors and ministry leaders.

ENDNOTES

1 David Miller, *God at Work: Your Christian Vocation in All of Life*, Wheaton, IL: Crossway, 2011, 49.

2 *The State of Pastors: How Today's Faith Leaders are Navigating Life and Leadership in an Age of Complexity*, Ventura, CA: Barna Group, 2017, 130.

3 Cornelius Plantinga, *Not the Way It's Supposed to Be: A Breviary of Sin*, Eerdmans, 1996, 10.

4 Humans are created with many aspects: bodily, emotional, rational, volitional, vocational, historical, social, economic, political, aesthetic, ethical, and more.

5 Nicholas Wolterstorff, *Educating for Shalom: Essays on Christian Higher Education*, ed. Clarence W. Joldersma and Gloria Goris Stronks, Eerdmans, 2004, 296.

6 To see the centrality of stewardship to the cultural mandate and its importance for economics, see Bob Goudzwaard, *Economic Stewardship Versus Capitalist Religion*, (unpublished notes of lectures given at Institute for Christian Studies, Toronto, 1972). It can be found online here: http://www.allofliferedeemed.co.uk/Goudzwaard/BG13.pdf

7 Hans Walter Wolff shows the importance of the words 'bless' and 'curse' Genesis 1-12 with a focus on the promise to Abraham in Gen 12:2-3. ("The Kerygma of the Yahwist," trans. Wilbur A. Benware, *Interpretation* 20, 2 (1966): 131-158. Creational blessing (Gen 1), the curse of sin (Gen 3-11), and the restoration of blessing (Gen 12). He observes that the fivefold use of the word 'bless' in Gen 12:2-3 is in direct response to the fivefold use of the word 'curse' in Gen 3-11.

8 Paul Marshall, with Lela Gilbert, *Heaven is Not My Home: Learning to Live in the Now of God's Creation*, Nashville: Word, 1998, 190.

9 Bob Goudzwaard refers to "three basic biblical rules:" 1) "that every man is serving god(s) in his life"; 2) "every man is transformed into an image of his god"; 3) "mankind creates and forms a structure of society in its own image." He goes on to elaborate: "In the development of human civilization, man forms, creates and changes the structure of his society, and in doing so he portrays in his work the intention of his own heart. He gives to the structure of that society something of his own image and likeness. In it he betrays something of his own lifestyle, of his own god. *Aid for the Overdeveloped West*, Toronto: Wedge Publishing Foundation, 1975, 14-15.

[10] N.T. Wright, *Scripture and the Authority of God* (rev. ed.), New York: HarperOne, 2013, 39.

[11] N.T. Wright, *Paul: In Fresh Perspective*, Minneapolis: Fortress Press, 2009, 109.

[12] N.T. Wright sees the so-called Sermon on the Mount as "a challenge to Israel to *be* Israel" and "an appeal to discover their true vocation as the eschatological people of YHWH." *Jesus and the Victory of God*, London: SPCK, 1996, 288-289.

[13] Some of the groups include, but are not limited, to the Kern Family Foundation, The Acton Institute, The Lily Endowment, The Templeton Foundation, Pew Research Center and many others.

[14] *Black's Law Dictionary* defines fiduciary as follows: "The term is derived from the Roman law and means (as a noun) a person holding the character of a trustee, or a character analogous to that of a trustee, in respect to the trust and confidence involved in it and the scrupulous good faith and candor which it requires. Thus, a person Is a fiduciary who is invested with rights and powers to be exercised for the benefit of another person. Svanoe v. Jurgens, 144 111.507, 33 N. E. 955; Stoll v. King, 8 How. Prac. (N. Y.) 299. As an adjective it means of the nature of a trust; having the characteristics of a trust; analogous to a trust; relating to or founded upon a trust or confidence."

[15] Karl Moore, "The End of Leadership At Least As We Know It," *Forbes Magazine*, October, 5 2012. https://www.forbes.com/sites/karlmoore/2012/10/05/the-end-of-leadership-at-least-as-we-know-it/#339b9cdd3078

[16] Barbara Kellerman, The End of Leadership.

[17] Moore, "The End of Leadership At Least As We Know It."

[18] A working definition of discipleship is best conveyed within the contemporary term "apprenticeship." An apprentice enters into an intentional relationship with a master in order to learn how to think, act and create from the same resources as their master. Identically a disciple of Jesus is learning how to live his or her life, within their specific contexts of work, family and relationships, as Jesus would live our life if he were in our identical contexts. WWJD (What Would Jesus Do) is helpful, but incomplete, when thinking about Christian discipleship. A modern disciple is not expected to live their life in the same way a first century, celibate, itinerant Jewish rabbi lived in and around ancient Palestine. Instead a contemporary disciple is learning from Jesus how to live their current life, with all the modern conveniences

and complexities that comprise our modern society, as Jesus would if he lived under similar circumstances.

[19] For a more complete investigation of the historical context that developed these theological concepts in American evangelicalism see chapter one of Gary Black, Jr, *The Theology of Dallas Willard: Discovering Protoevangelical Faith,* Pickwick Pub, 2013.

[20] Just a few instances are noted here. https://www.npr.org/2018/01/24/580193284/amid-metoo-evangelicals-grapple-with-misconduct-in-churchtoo , http://time.com/5076537/evangelical-women-church-speak-out-metoo/ , https://www.christianitytoday.com/women/2017/october/unsettling-truth-behind-me-too-movement-harvey-weinstein.html, and https://www.csmonitor.com/USA/Politics/2018/0420/Churches-struggle-with-their-MeToo-moment .

[21] Dallas Willard, *Renovation of the Heart: Putting on the Character of Christ,* (Colorado Springs, CO; Nav Press, 2002), 38.

[22] https://discipleshipdynamics.com.

[23] Aristotle, *Nicomachean Ethics,* Translated by Martin Ostwald, Upper Saddle River, NJ; Prentice Hall, 1999, Book VIII.

[24] As an example of the kind or type of friendship I am suggesting here, we should consider the role of a "sponsor" in the Alcoholics Anonymous recovery organization or many of the other substance abuse recovery organizations. The analogy is not perfect to the kind of Aristotelian friendship I am suggesting. But it is a close second and there have been good research conducted on the effectiveness of the sponsor relationship to sobriety. For instance, see Paul J. P. Whelan, E. Jane Marshall, David M. Ball, Keith Humphreys, "The Role of AA Sponsors: A Pilot Study" in *Alcohol and Alcoholism,* Vol. 44, 4, July 2009, 416–422.

[25] A good explanation and introduction to the concept of a Rule of Life that I have used in some of my classes over the years comes from the C.S. Lewis Institute. See http://www.cslewisinstitute.org/webfm_send/338.

[26] http://www.cslewisinstitute.org/webfm_send/338.

[27] http://www.chicagotribune.com/sports/international/ct-larry-nassar-gymnastics-sentencing-20180124-story.html

[28] Op-Ed, *The New York Times,* January 26, 2018. https://www.nytimes.com/2018/01/26/opinion/sunday/larry-nassar-rachael-denhollander.html

[29] https://www.detroitnews.com/story/news/local/michigan/2018/01/24/rachael-den-hollander-larry-nassar-statement/10978198/

[30] All references from the New International Version.

[31] See Scott Rae, "Economics in the Bible," in Adam Joyce and Greg Forster, ed., *Economic Wisdom for Churches*, Oikonomia Network, 2017. Other resources on connecting the Bible's witness with our economic life today include Tom Nelson, *The Economics of Neighborly Love*, InterVarsity, 2017; and Brent Waters, *Just Capitalism*, Westminster John Knox, 2016.

[32] See Peter Phan, Message of the Fathers of the Church (Social Thought), Michael Glazier, 1983; and Helen Rhee, Loving the Poor, Saving the Rich, Baker, 2012.

[33] See Stephen Grabill, "Editor's Introduction," ed. Stephen Grabill, *A Sourcebook in Late-Scholastic Monetary Theory*, Acton Institute, 2007; and Greg Forster, *The Contested Public Square*, InterVarsity Press, 2008.

[34] See Martin Luther's "Disputation on the Power and Efficacy of Indulgences," otherwise known as the 95 Theses, available at: http://www.luther.de/en/95thesen.html; see also Greg Forster, *The Church on Notice*, Center for Transformational Churches, 2017.

[35] See, for example, Matthew Tuininga, "Why Calvin Had Good News for the Poor," Gospel Coalition, October 26, 2016; see also David Hall and Matthew Burton, *Calvin and Commerce*, P&R Publishing, 2009.

[36] See David Wright, *How God Makes the World a Better Place*, Acton Institute, 2012.

[37] See Greg Forster, "Why Jonathan Edwards Saw Economic Justice as a Gospel Concern," Gospel Coalition, August 22, 2016.

[38] Martin Luther King Jr., "I Have a Dream," delivered at the March on Washington for Jobs and Freedom, August 28, 1963. See also his classic faith and work speech, which raises issues of economic justice: Martin Luther King Jr., "What Is Your Life's Blueprint?" delivered at Barratt Junior High School in Philadelphia, October 26, 1967.

[39] On this history see Greg Forster, "Opportunity: What Does Justice Require?" in Adam Joyce and Greg Forster, ed., *Economic Wisdom for Churches*, Oikonomia Network, 2017; for a more specific look at the expansion of economic rights two centuries ago see P.J. Hill, "Made for Dignity," in Drew Cleveland and Greg Forster, ed., *The Pastor's Guide to Fruitful Work and Economic Wisdom*, Made to Flourish, 2012.

[40] See George Fredrickson, *Racism: A Short History*, Princeton University Press, 2002.

[41] Nick Shultz, *Home Economics*, American Enterprise Institute, 2013.

[42] Jennifer Roback Morse, *Love and Economics*, Ruth Institute, 2008.

[43] There are an estimated 553,742 people in the United States experiencing homelessness on a given night, according to the most recent national point-in-time estimate (January 2017). This represents a rate of approximately 17 people experiencing homelessness per every 10,000 people in the general population. tps://endhomelessness.org/homelessness-in-america/homelessness-statistics/state-of-homelessness-report/

[44] Craig Van Gelder, *The Essence of The Church*, Grand Rapids: Baker Books, 2000, 131.

[45] 1 Timothy 3:15.

[46] Matthew 16:18b.

[47] The Greek word is "ekklesia" and has the idea of calling out.

[48] A term increasingly used of commercial enterprises in our time is "glocal," capturing the sense of having a local footprint as well as a global reach. "Glocal" might well be used to describe the church as well in capturing its multifaceted mission and influence.

[49] For example, in writing to a particular local church at Ephesus, the apostle Paul strongly affirms the universal church. Speaking of Christ, Paul declares, "*And He put all things in subjection under his feet and gave Him as head over all things to the church, which is his body, the fullness of Him who fills all in all,*" (Eph 1:22-23).

[50] Miroslav Volf, *After Our Likeness: The Church as the Image of the* Trinity, Eerdmans, 1998, 25. See also Volf, *137* and 1 Corinthians 14:23.

[51] Acts 1:8.

[52] Ephesians 4:11-16; Romans 12:3-8; 1 Corinthians 12.

[53] Dietrich Bonhoeffer, *Life Together*, Harper & Row, 1954, 21.

[54] For more elaboration on these common consumer metaphors of the church see Tom Nelson's, *Ekklesia, Rediscovering God's Design for The Church*, CrossTraining Publishers, 2009, 12-14.

[55] Clowney notes, "Paul Minear found no fewer than ninety-six figures and analogies that are applied to the church in the New Testament. Some figures have become master metaphors, shaping the understanding of the church." Edmund Clowney, The Church, InterVarsity, 1994, 71-72.

[56] 1 Timothy 3:15.

[57] 1 Corinthians 3:9.

[58] 1 Peter 2:4.

[59] 1 Peter 2:9.

[60] Curt Thompson, *Anatomy of The Soul,* Tyndale, 2010, 244.

[61] Genesis 1:26-28.

[62] While there are many spiritual disciplines, I like to refer to the foundational ones as the five smooth stones of solitude, study, prayer, fasting and service. Dallas Willard has persuasively articulated the transformational role of spiritual disciplines both on an individual and corporate level. I highly recommend his outstanding books, *Spirit of the Disciplines* and *Renovation of the Heart.*

[63] 2 Peter 1:5a.

[64] Charles Taylor speaks of "the imminent frame" of all reality being restricted to the here and now as a defining characteristic of much of the Western world in late modernity. Charles Taylor, *A Secular Age,* Harvard University Press, 2007.

[65] Jesus' words in Matthew 5:13-16 frame his follower's influential effect of salt and light in a culture. Jesus uses a first person plural pronoun emphasizing the collective nature of his apprentices and concludes by saying, "*In the same way, let your light shine before others, so that they may see your good works and give glory to your Father who is in heaven.*"

[66] See research at Institute for Family Studies, https://ifstudies.org/Of particular importance is the work of University of Virginia professor Brad Wilcox. See also Tyler J. VanderWeele and his research on church attendance and human flourishing.

[67] See Tom Nelson's book, *Work Matters*, which makes the case for a robust vocational theology at the heart of the church and its gospel mission in the world.

[68] A church committed to true whole life discipleship not only connects Sunday to Monday, but also brings Monday into Sunday. Pastoral prayers focus on Monday life. Benedictions connect with Monday life. Sermons utilize illustrations and tilt applications toward Monday work. One example of an increasing common liturgy is a corporate worship segment called This Time Tomorrow. During the gathered corporate worship service, an individual member will be interviewed about what God has called them to do this time tomorrow. All callings and forms of work paid

and unpaid are affirmed. Three questions are asked a parishioner. First, what will you be doing this time tomorrow? Second, What are the joys and challenges where God has placed you? Third, How can we pray for you? At the conclusion of these three questions, the congregant is prayed for and commissioned for the work God has called them to do throughout the week.

[69] See Tom Nelson's book, *The Economics of Neighborly Love* that makes the persuasive case for understanding biblical teaching as a call to productivity and fruitfulness. A church for Monday embraces a strong integration of faith, work and economic wisdom.

[70] A local church as an influential economic actor in a community is called the halo effect. A first-of-its-kind analysis of religion's socio-economic value shows that faith-related businesses and institutions add more than $1 trillion to the U.S. economy. If U.S. religion was its own country, it would be the 15th largest economy in the world, according to a new study that presents faith in financial terms. Religion-related businesses and institutions, as well as houses of worship, bring in more revenue each year than Google, Apple and Amazon combined, contributing around $1.2 trillion annually to America's GDP, according to "The Socio-economic Contributions of Religion to American Society: An Empirical Analysis," published in the *Interdisciplinary Journal of Research on Religion*. https://www.deseretnews. com/article/865662454/Economic-impact-of-religion-New-report-says-its-worth-more-than-Google-Apple-and-Amazon-combined.html.

[71] For further reading on the importance of the local church and economic flourishing, I would highly recommend, *The Economics of Neighborly Love*, InterVarsity, 2017; *Redeeming Capitalism*, Kenneth J. Barnes, Eerdmans, 2018; Brent Waters, *Just Capitalism*, Westminster John Knox Press, 2016; and Bruno Roche, Jay Jacob, *Completing Capitalism*, Berret-Koehler Publishers, 2017.

[72] The prophet Jeremiah calls God's covenant people exiled in the pagan city of Babylon to seek the welfare or shalom of the city. The Hebrew idea of shalom captures the comprehensive nature of human wellbeing both as individuals and society as a whole. Shalom is the world reflecting its original creation design and desire, the world as it ought to be. See Jeremiah 29:4-7. Note the emphasis Jeremiah places on economic well-being.

[73] Ephesians 5:25-33.

[74] Revelation 19:7-8.

[75] MacIntyre, Alasdair. *After Virtue: A Study in Moral Theory*, (3rd ed.), Notre Dame: University of Notre Dame Press, 2007, 216.

[76] Mentioned by a Florida pastor, June 2014.